English

phrases
explained
in English

Intermediate
Level

英語を英語で理解する

英英
英熟語
中級編

ジャパンタイムズ出版 英語出版編集部 &
ロゴポート 編

英英
英単語
SERIES

the japan times 出版

はじめに

　本書は『英語を英語で理解する　英英英単語®』シリーズの姉妹編です。英語学習の基礎となる、中級レベルの約500の熟語を取り上げています。前半でイディオムを、後半で句動詞を取り上げています*。

　既刊の『英英英単語®』シリーズは、英語による見出し語の語義説明を掲載することで、英語のニュアンスを正しく捉え、かつ自分の考えを平易な言葉で伝える力をつけることを目的とした、新しい単語集でした。幸い、このシリーズは多くの方に好意的に迎えていただくことができましたが、英文を正しく理解するためには、単語だけでなく、熟語についての理解も欠かすことはできません。そこで誕生したのが、本書『英語を英語で理解する 英英英熟語 中級編』です。

　Longman Dictionary of Contemporary EnglishやOxford Advanced Learner's Dictionaryといった学習者用の英英辞典は、平易な語句で語義を説明しているので、見出し語句のニュアンスが捉えやすく、言いたいことをシンプルな語句で表現する際の参考にもなる、優れた英語学習ツールです。一方、辞書であるために情報が多すぎて語彙学習には使いづらく、語義説明の理解が不十分だと英和辞典を引き直す手間がかかってしまう、というデメリットもあります。

　『英英英単語®／英英英熟語』シリーズは、こうした問題をクリアすべく作られています。本書では、大学受験生や一般の英語学習者の役に立つ中級レベルの約500の熟語を厳選しました。そして、各種の英英辞典を参考に、ネイティブが書きおろしたオリジナルの英語

の語義説明と、見出しの熟語の典型的な使い方を示した例文を付けました。学習効率の向上のため、見出しの熟語と例文の訳、さらに英語の語義説明の訳も掲載しています（語義説明の訳の掲載は、今回の新たな試みです）。また、単語編同様、類義表現、反意表現、語法情報も掲載しています。

　このように、本書を学習すれば、あらゆる英語学習者に必要な初級レベルの熟語を英語で理解し、その具体的な使い方を知ることができるようになっています。

　本書を読み込み、そして使い倒してください。少しずつ頭の中に英語回路が形成され、一般的な語彙集では手に入らない熟語のニュアンスの知識とパラフレージング力が身につくでしょう。
　本書が読者の皆さまの語彙力向上の一助になれば、これに過ぎる喜びはありません。

編者

＊イディオムと句動詞の区別は、Oxford Advanced Learner's Dictionaryなどの英英辞典の分類を参考にしています。

目次

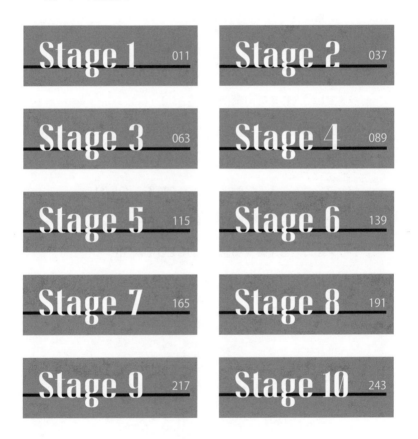

ビジュアルでとらえる句動詞

ナレーション：Chris Koprowski／Jennifer Okano
録音・編集：ELEC録音スタジオ

カバー・本文デザイン：竹内雄二
イラスト：矢戸優人
DTP組版：清水裕久（Pesco Paint）

本書の構成と使い方

　本書では、中級レベルの約500の熟語を10のSTAGE に分けて掲載しています。STAGE 1～5ではイディオムを、STAGE 6～10では句動詞を取り上げています。

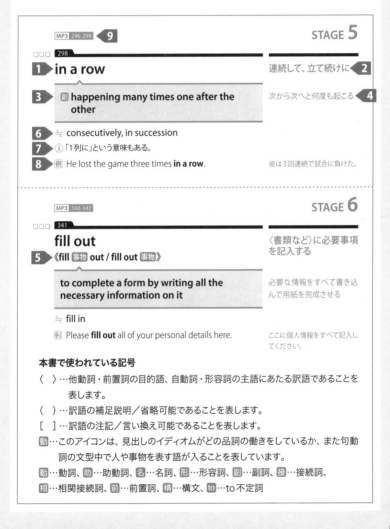

本書で使われている記号

〈　〉…他動詞・前置詞の目的語、自動詞・形容詞の主語にあたる訳語であることを
　　　表します。

(　)…訳語の補足説明/省略可能であることを表します。

[　]…訳語の注記/言い換え可能であることを表します。

動…このアイコンは、見出しのイディオムがどの品詞の働きをしているか、また句動
　　詞の文型中で人や事物を表す語が入ることを表しています。

動…動詞、助…助動詞、名…名詞、形…形容詞、副…副詞、接…接続詞、
相…相関接続詞、前…前置詞、構…構文、to…to不定詞

1 見出しの熟語

米つづりを採用しています。

2 見出しの熟語の訳

見出しの熟語の訳です。赤フィルターで隠すことができます。

3 品詞および英語の語義説明

見出しのイディオムがどの品詞の働きをしているか、また熟語の語義を英語で説明しています。特によく使われる語義、学習者が覚えておくと役に立つ語義を選んで掲載しています。

※ 本来、熟語に品詞があるわけではないので、大まかな目安としてお考えください。便宜上、文の形をとるものは構、to不定詞と同じ働きをするものはtoとしています。

※ 大きく語義の異なるものは一般の辞書では別見出しにすることがありますが、本書では適宜1つの見出しにまとめています。

※ 語義説明では英英辞書にならい、総称人称のyou（人一般を表すyou）、singular they（he or sheの代用）を使っている場合があります。

4 英語の語義説明の訳

英語の語義説明の訳です。赤フィルターで隠すことができます。

5 文型

句動詞の文型を示しています。

6 類義表現と反意表現

≒の後ろに掲載されているのは見出しの熟語の類義表現、⇔の後ろに掲載されているのは見出しの熟語の反意表現です。

7 注記

①の後ろには、見出しの熟語の語法、関連語などの補足情報を掲載しています。

8 例文と訳

見出しの熟語を使った例文とその訳です。英文中の見出し相当部分は太字になっています。訳は赤フィルターで隠すことができます。

9 音声のトラック番号

付属音声には各項目の見出しの熟語、英語の語義説明、例文（英文）

が収録されています。音声はアプリまたはPCでダウンロードすることがで
きます。ご利用方法は010ページをご覧ください。

章末ボキャブラリーチェック

各STAGEの終わりに、確認のための問題を用意しています。赤フィルターでペー
ジを隠し、本文にあった語義説明を見て、ヒントを参考に見出しの熟語を答えま
しょう。間違えた場合は元のページに戻って復習しましょう。

コラム：ビジュアルでとらえる句動詞

本書で取り上げた多くの意味を持つ9つの句動詞を、ビジュアルを交えて説明
しています。基本的な動詞や副詞／前置詞をイメージでとらえる習慣をつけると、
複数の意味を理解する助けとなります。

音声のご利用案内

本書の音声は、スマートフォン（アプリ）やパソコンを通じてMP3形式でダウンロードし、ご利用いただくことができます。

 スマートフォン

1. ジャパンタイムズ出版の音声アプリ「OTO Navi」をインストール

2. OTO Naviで本書を検索

3. OTO Naviで音声をダウンロードし、再生

3秒早送り・早戻し、繰り返し再生などの便利機能つき。学習にお役立てください。

 パソコン

1. ブラウザからジャパンタイムズ出版のサイト「BOOK CLUB」にアクセス
https://bookclub.japantimes.co.jp/book/b613762.html

2.「ダウンロード」ボタンをクリック

3. 音声をダウンロードし、iTunesなどに取り込んで再生

※音声はzipファイルを展開（解凍）してご利用ください。

Stage 1

There's no time like the present.
思い立ったが吉日。

☐☐☐ **001**

at any cost

何としても

🔤 used to say something has to be done no matter how difficult it may be

どんなに困難であっても何かをしなければならないと述べるのに使われる

≒ at all costs

📝 This product has to be a success **at any cost**.

この商品は何としても成功させなければならない。

☐☐☐ **002**

out of date

時代遅れの、すたれた

📏 ① no longer useful or effective

もはや役に立たない、あるいは効力を持たない

≒ outdated

⇔ up to date

ⓘ 名詞を修飾するときは out-of-date の形。

📝 This software is so **out of date**.

このソフトは、とても時代遅れだ。

〈情報が〉古くなった

② no longer recent and potentially incorrect

もはや最新ではなく、間違っている可能性がある

≒ outdated

📝 Even though it was just printed, this information is already **out of date**.

印刷されたばかりとはいえ、この情報はすでに古い。

期限切れの、失効した

③ no longer legally acceptable

もはや法的に許容されない

📝 On his way to the airport, he realized his passport was **out of date**.

空港に行く途中、彼はパスポートが期限切れであることに気がついた。

□□□ 003

that is (to say)

つまり、正確に言うと

副 ① used to give more specific information about someone or something just mentioned

言及されたばかりの誰かまたは何かについて、さらに具体的な情報を提供するのに使われる

例 They, **that is to say** John and Bobby, decided they won't be coming to the dance.

彼ら、つまりジョンとボビーは、ダンスに行かないことにした。

もっとも（〜の話だが）

② used to give information that affects something previously mentioned

前に述べた何かに影響を及ぼす情報を提供するのに使われる

例 I can give you a ride to the airport—**that is**, if you still want one.

空港まで車で送るよ。もっとも君がまだそうしてほしいならの話だけど。

□□□ 004

in case of

〜の場合には

前 if something happens

何かが起きたら

≒ in the event of

ⓘ 公的な通知で使われることが多い。

例 **In case of** cancellation, please show your ticket at the counter to receive a full refund.

キャンセルの場合は、カウンターでチケットをご提示いただければ、全額返金いたします。

□□□ 005

go your own way

自分の思いどおりにやる

動 to do what you want regardless of what someone else has said

ほかの誰かが何と言おうと、自分のしたいことをする

例 Not all young people are ready to **go their own way** after finishing high school.

すべての若者が高校を卒業して自分の道を歩む準備ができているわけではない。

005句

□□□ **006**

take your place

席に着く、
所定の位置に着く

励 ① to go to where you are supposed to be

いるべき場所に行く

例 All of the wedding guests **took their places** when the music started.

音楽が始まると、結婚式の招待客はみんな自分の席に着いた。

（ある地位などに）
名を連ねる

② to accept your status in society

社会における立場を受け入れる

例 The library has **taken its place** as top teen hangout spot in town.

その図書館は、町で一番の10代の若者のたまり場になっている。

□□□ **007**

in less than no time

あっという間に

副 so quickly that it is surprising

驚くほど早く

≒ in next to no time, in no time

例 The server brought out a replacement bottle **in less than no time**.

給仕係は、あっという間に替えのボトルを持ってきた。

□□□ **008**

by no means

まったく～ない

副 in no way

決して～ない

≒ not at all

例 Although it has stopped raining, it is **by no means** certain that the game will still be held.

雨はやんだが、試合が行われるかどうかは決して確実ではない。

□□□ 009

in light of

〜を考慮して

前 ① after thinking about something

何かについて考えた後で

例 **In light of** this new data, we may want to alter our teaching methodology.

この新しいデータに鑑みると、私たちは教え方を変えたほうがいいかもしれない。

〜を受けて、踏まえて

② because of something

何かのために

例 **In light of** some unexpected funding issues, we have decided to cancel this year's summer festival.

予期せぬ資金調達の問題のため、私たちは今年の夏祭りを中止することにした。

□□□ 010

in the short run

短期的には、差し当たっては

副 in the near future

近い将来に

≒ in the short term

⇔ in the long run

例 Although the policy might have some negative effects **in the short run**, overall it will be good for the economy.

この政策は短期的には悪影響を与えるかもしれないが、全体としては経済によい影響を与えるだろう。

□□□ 011

keep your temper

平静を保つ、怒りを抑える

動 to control your anger and stay calm

怒りを抑えて冷静でいる

≒ keep your cool

⇔ lose your temper

例 **Keep your temper** and we can figure out a solution together.

落ち着いてください。そうすれば一緒に解決策を見つけられます。

011句

□□□ **012**

under pressure

（気体や液体などが）
加圧されて

形 ① **forced to stay in a container in an amount that will make it escape the container with force when opened**

開けたときにそこから勢い
よくあふれ出てしまうほど
の量を、容器に押し込めら
れて

例 This canister contains gas **under pressure**.

この容器には加圧された気体
が入っている。

（精神的な）圧力を受け
て、プレッシャーを受けて

② **being forced or urged to do something**

何かをするように強制され
て、あるいは促されて

例 The CEO is **under** increasing **pressure** to make a statement about his alleged affair.

CEOには、不倫疑惑について
声明を出すよう圧力が高まって
いる。

□□□ **013**

for all I know

（よくは知らないが）
もしかしたら

副 **used to say that you do not know much about something**

何かについてあまり知らな
いと述べるのに使われる

例 She could already be in Las Vegas **for all I know**.

もしかしたら、彼女はもうラス
ベガスにいるかもしれない。

□□□ **014**

in addition to

〜に加えて、〜のほかに

前 **used to add more information to what has already been said**

すでに述べたことにさらに
情報を付け加えるのに使わ
れる

例 **In addition to** being convoluted, your proposal is incomplete.

あなたの提案は入り組んでい
るうえに、不完全です。

□□□ **015**

as many as

（後に数詞を伴って）〜
もの、ほど多くの

**形 used to emphasize just how large a
number is**

数がどれだけ大きいかを強
調するのに使われる

例 There are **as many as** 30 deer in that field right now.

今、その畑には30頭もの鹿が
いる。

□□□ **016**

give way to

〜に取って代わられる、
移行する

動 ① to be replaced by something

何かに置き替えられる

例 Her anger quickly **gave way to** exhaustion and
feelings of defeat.

彼女の怒りは、すぐに疲れと敗
北感に変わった。

〜に譲歩する、屈する

**② to stop resisting someone or
something and agree to do what you
do not want to do**

誰かまたは何かに抵抗する
のをやめて、したくないこと
をするのに同意する

≒ give in to

例 Despite everything, she was unwilling to **give way to**
the demands of the public.

何が何でも、彼女は世間の要
求に屈しようとはしなかった。

〜に道を譲る

**③ to let someone or something be or go
first**

誰かまたは何かが先にいる
ようにする、あるいは先に
行かせる

≒ yield to

ⓘ イギリス英語。

例 There are several rules about when you have to **give
way to** another vehicle in an intersection.

交差点でほかの車に道を譲ら
なければならないときには、い
くつかの規則がある。

016句

□□□ **017**

in the presence of

〈人〉のいるところで

前 used to describe being in the same place as another person

ほかの人と同じ場所にいることを述べるのに使われる

≒ around

ⓘ in *someone's* presence の形でも使われる。

例 You shall not act in that manner **in the presence of** the Queen.

女王のいる前でそのような振る舞いをしてはならない。

□□□ **018**

at a distance

少し離れて、
距離を置いて

副 used to talk about a situation in which something is far away from you in space or time

何かが自分から空間的または時間的に離れているという状況について話すのに使われる

ⓘ from a distance とも言う。

例 **At a distance**, the mountains looked like the face of an old man.

遠くから見ると、その山は老人の顔のように見えた。

□□□ **019**

up in the air

宙に浮いて、未定で

形 uncertain and undecided

不確実で未定の

例 Their plans are all **up in the air** because of the weather.

天候のため、彼らの計画はすべて未定だ。

□□□ **020**

one of these days

近いうちに、そのうちに

副 at some point in the future

将来のある時点で

≒ one day

例 **One of these days** we should really go visit your grandmother.

そのうち、本当におばあちゃんに会いに行こうね。

□□□ 021

take hold of

～をつかむ

動 to begin holding someone or something

誰かまたは何かをつかみ始める

≒ catch, get, grab

例 She **took hold of** the railing to steady herself.

彼女は転ばないように手すりにつかまった。

□□□ 022

in return for

～のお返しに、お礼に

前 showing thanks to someone or paying them for something they have done

誰かに感謝を示して、あるいはしてくれたことに対してお金を払って

例 Kazu brought over some fish **in return for** the vegetables we had given him.

ガズは、私たちがあげた野菜のお礼に魚を持ってきてくれた。

□□□ 023

up to date

最新(式)の、流行している

形 ① modern or fashionable

今風の、あるいは流行の

⇔ out of date

例 Bernadette always tries to keep her wardrobe **up to date**.

バーナデットはいつもワードローブに流行の服をそろえておくようにしている。

最新情報の入った

② including all the most recent information

最新情報すべてを含んでいる

例 We have made sure that all of our pamphlets are **up to date**.

私たちは、パンフレットがすべて最新情報であることを確かめた。

023句

□□□ 024

on the part of

〜の側で、〜によって

前 made or done by someone

誰かによって作られた、または行われた

ⓘ on *someone's* part の形でも使われる。

例 It was all just a mistake **on the part of** the secretary.

それはすべて単に秘書のミスだった。

□□□ 025

come to light

明らかになる

動 to become known to other people

ほかの人に知られるようになる

≒ be brought to light

例 Many things have **come to light** since his private journals were discovered.

彼の私的な日記が発見されて以来、多くのことが明るみに出ている。

□□□ 026

not to mention

〜は言うまでもなく

接 used to introduce extra information and provide emphasis

追加の情報を導入し、強調するのに使われる

≒ in addition to, let alone

例 We can't afford to go, **not to mention** the fact that I wouldn't be able to miss work.

私が仕事を休めないのはもちろん、出かける余裕もない。

□□□ 027

for a change

いつもと違って、たまには

副 instead of what usually is done or happens

通常行われることや起こることではなく

例 It would be great if you did the laundry **for a change**.

たまにはあなたが洗濯をしてくれるとうれしいです。

□□□ 028

in exchange for

~と引き換えに

前 given because of something that has been given to you

自分に与えられた何かのおかげで与えられた

例 What did they offer **in exchange for** your services?

彼らはあなたの尽力と引き換えに何を提供しましたか。

□□□ 029

free of charge

無料で

副 without needing to pay any money

お金を一切払う必要なしに

例 You may enter this event **free of charge**.

このイベントには無料で参加できます。

□□□ 030

may as well *do*

~したほうがよい（ではないか）

助 ① used to tell someone they should do something since there is no reason not to

しない理由がないのだから何かをするべきだと誰かに言うのに使われる

ⓘ might as well の形でも使われる。

例 You've got nothing to lose, so you **may as well** try it.

失うものは何もないんだから、やってみればいいんじゃない？

~するのと同然だ

② used to say something else could have been done to achieve the same result

同じ結果を得るのにほかの何かをすることもできたと述べるのに使われる

例 His accent is so strong, he **may as well** be speaking a foreign language.

彼のなまりはとても強くて、外国語を話しているのも同然だ。

030句

□□□ 031

in person

（代理や手紙でなく）直接、対面で

🔲 **used to say a person is actually at a place**

ある人が実際にある場所にいることを言うために使われる

例 All interviews at our company are conducted **in person**.

当社の面接はすべて対面で行います。

□□□ 032

for the time being

当面、差し当たって

🔲 **for a short period of time that is not permanent**

永続的ではない短い間

例 **For the time being**, we are asking all residents to limit their use of electricity.

当面の間、住民の皆さまには電力使用の制限をお願いいたします。

□□□ 033

on the contrary

それどころか、むしろ

🔲 **used to say the opposite of what was previously said is true**

前に言われたことの逆が真実であると言うのに使われる

≒ quite the contrary

例 Happy? **On the contrary**, my coworkers are upset that they didn't think of the idea first.

喜んでいる？ それどころか、同僚たちはそのアイデアを最初に思いつかなかったことに動揺しています。

□□□ 034

on the whole

全体的に見て；概して

🔲 **used to say something generally**

何かを一般化して言うのに使われる

例 **On the whole**, this grocery store doesn't sell a lot of meat products.

概して、この食料品店では肉類をあまりたくさん売っていない。

☐☐☐ 035

put an end to

〈よくないことなど〉を終わらせる

動 to stop something from continuing because it is not good

よくないという理由で何かが続くのを止める

≒ put a stop to

例 When they started hitting each other, their mother quickly **put an end to** the fight.

彼らが殴り合いを始めると、母親はすぐにけんかをやめさせた。

☐☐☐ 036

be all eyes

注意深く見る、注視する

動 to watch someone or something carefully and with a lot of interest

誰かまたは何かを、注意深く、強い関心を持って見る

例 The students **were all eyes** as the man lifted the iguana out of its cage.

男性がイグアナをかごから持ち上げて出すと、生徒たちはじっと見た。

☐☐☐ 037

put yourself in *someone's* shoes

〜の立場に立ってみる

動 to imagine yourself in another person's situation

自分がほかの人の状況にいるのを想像する

例 If you **put yourself in her shoes**, I imagine you'll be able to understand a little better.

彼女の立場に立ってみれば、あなたにももう少し理解できるだろうと思います。

☐☐☐ 038

run the risk of *doing*

〜する危険を冒す

動 to be or put yourself in a situation where something bad could happen

何か悪いことが起こり得る状況にある、またはそのような状況に身を置く

例 If we raise prices, we'll **run the risk of** upsetting our existing customers.

値上げをすると、既存の顧客を怒らせてしまうリスクがある。

038句

□□□ **039**

find fault with

~のあら探しをする、
~に文句を言う

動 to look for and point out problems in someone or something, especially unfairly and repeatedly

特に不当に、繰り返し、誰
かまたは何かの問題点を探
し、指摘する

例 It seems like you **find fault with** anything that he does.

あなたは何かにつけ彼のやる
ことのあら探しをしているよう
に見える。

□□□ **040**

take it for granted that

…を当然のことと考える

動 to not properly notice or appreciate someone or something

誰かまたは何かについて、
適切に言及したり評価した
りしない

例 You should never **take it for granted that** your parents are around.

親がそばにいることを当然だと
思うべきではない。

□□□ **041**

in order that

…するために

接 so that something can happen or be done

何かが起きる、あるいは行
われるように

例 Please leave your key here **in order that** we can move your car if needed.

必要があればこちらでお客
さまのお車を移動できるように、
鍵をお預けください。

□□□ **042**

over and over (again)

何度も、再三

副 used to say something is done many times

何かが何度も行われると述
べるのに使われる

≒ repeatedly

例 The man hit the drum **over and over again**.

男性は、何度も何度もドラムを
たたいた。

□□□ 043

only too

とても、非常に

副 ① used to say you are willing to do something

喜んで何かをすると述べる
のに使われる

例 We'd be **only too** happy to show you around the grounds when you are free this afternoon.

今日の午後、お時間のあるとき
に、敷地の周辺を喜んでご案
内させていただきます。

残念ながら

② used to say you wish that the situation was different

状況が違うものであってほ
しかったと述べるのに使わ
れる

例 We are **only too** aware of the consequences an oil leak may have.

私たちは残念ながら、オイル漏
れがどのような結果をもたらし
得るかわかっている。

□□□ 044

for all

～にもかかわらず

前 in spite of something

何かにもかかわらず

≒ despite

例 **For all** her grumbling, it looks like she actually had a really good time.

彼女は文句ばかり言っていた
が、実際にはとても楽しんでい
たようだ。

～（がわずかであるこ
と）を考えると

接 used to say that something is not important or interesting to you or someone else

自分またはほかの誰かに
とって、何かが重要でない
または興味がないと言うた
めに使われる

例 We could paint the house hot pink, **for all** I care!

家をショッキングピンクに塗ろう
がどうしようが私は構わない。

044句

□□□ **045**

take advantage of

〈機会など〉を利用する、生かす

動 ① to use a situation to do or get what you want

したいことをする、または欲しいものを手に入れるために、ある状況を使う

≒ make good use of

例 Ross **took advantage of** the low interest rates to invest in several properties.

ロスは低金利を生かし、いくつかの不動産に投資した。

〈人〉をだます

② to treat someone unfairly to get what you want

欲しいものを手に入れるために誰かを不当に扱う

≒ exploit

例 The company has been accused of **taking advantage of** people with limited financial education.

その会社は、限られた金融教育しか受けていない人々を食い物にしていると非難されてきた。

～を悪用する

③ to use something unfairly to get what you want

欲しいものを手に入れるために何かを不当に使う

≒ exploit

例 She **took advantage of** a loophole that allowed her to get the discount multiple times.

彼女は、何度も割引を受けることを可能にする抜け道を悪用した。

□□□ **046**

by any chance

もしかして

副 used to politely ask whether something is true

何かが真実かどうかを礼儀正しく尋ねるのに使われる

例 Would you happen to have apple juice **by any chance**?

もしかして、リンゴジュースがあったりする?

□□□ 047

from time to time

たまに、ときどき

副 sometimes, but not regularly

ときどきではあるが、定期的
ではなく

≒ occasionally, once in a while, on occasions

例 Kathy visits her sister in the city **from time to time**.

キャシーはたまに都会に住む
妹を訪ねる。

□□□ 048

in that

…という点で、
…という理由で

接 used to start explaining in what way something is true

何かが、どのように真実で
あるかを説明し始めるのに
使われる

≒ because

例 We were lucky **in that** none of us got sick during our month in Europe.

ヨーロッパでの1か月間、誰一
人病気にならなかったのは幸
運だった。

□□□ 049

make yourself understood

自分の言いたいことを
相手に伝える

動 to succeed in getting someone to understand what you are saying

自分の言っていることを誰
かに理解してもらうことに
成功する

例 Tom struggled to **make himself understood** despite significant effort.

かなりの努力をしたにもかか
わらず、トムは自分のことを理
解してもらうのに苦労した。

□□□ 050

needless to say

言うまでもなく

副 used to emphasize what you are saying is obvious

自分の言っていることが明
らかであることを強調する
のに使われる

≒ of course, obviously

050句

例 **Needless to say**, she wasn't welcome at the restaurant anymore.

言うまでもなく、もう彼女はそ
のレストランに歓迎されていな
かった。

□□□ 051

at *someone's* convenience

〈人〉の都合のいいときに

副 at a time or place that is suitable for someone

誰かに都合のいい時間または場所で

例 I'd prefer to meet **at your convenience**, so please tell me some times that are good for you.

ご都合に合わせてお会いしたいと思いますので、いい時間をいくつか教えてください。

□□□ 052

to go

残して

形 ① still remaining before something happens

何かが起こる前にまだ残っている

例 There's only one more year **to go** until I can retire.

退職できるまでもうあと1年だけだ。

あと

② still needing to be done or dealt with in order to be finished

完了するために、まだ行う必要がある、または対処する必要がある

例 Just two more sales **to go**, and then we'll have hit our monthly quota.

あと2回売れさえすれば、われわれは月間のノルマを達成できる。

持ち帰り用に

副 (of a food order) to be taken away from the restaurant and eaten somewhere else

（食べ物の注文について）飲食店から持ち出され、別の場所で食べられる

例 Aside from our main order, I'd also like to order a small cheese pizza **to go**.

メインの注文とは別に、持ち帰りでチーズピザのSサイズをお願いします。

□□□ 053

so to speak

いわば、まるで

副 used to emphasize you are saying something in an unusual or funny way

自分が、いつもとは違うまたは面白い言い方で何かを述べていることを強調するのに使われる

例 We must open the doors to employment, **so to speak**, that are currently closed to our homeless population.

私たちは、現状ホームレスの人たちに閉ざされている、いわば雇用の扉を開かなければならない。

□□□ 054

to say nothing of

〜は言うまでもなく

to used to introduce an additional fact after others have already been mentioned

ほかの事実についてすでに言及した後に、さらなる事実を導入するのに使われる

≒ not to mention

例 Being late on your credit card payments causes late fees, **to say nothing of** its effect on your credit rating.

クレジットカードの支払いが遅れると延滞金が発生するうえ、信用評価に影響することは言うまでもない。

□□□ 055

to your heart's content

心ゆくまで、思う存分

副 as much as you want

好きなだけ

例 Eat **to your heart's content** at our gourmet all-you-can-eat buffet.

当店の食べ放題のグルメビュッフェで心ゆくまでお食事をお楽しみください。

□□□ 056

at the expense of

〜を犠牲にして

前 in a way that does damage to someone or something

誰かまたは何かに損害を与える方法で

例 We were able to finish in time for the launch, but **at the expense of** everyone's sleep.

私たちは発売に間に合わせることができたが、全員の睡眠時間を犠牲にした。

056句

057

day in and day out

来る日も来る日も

副 every day for a long period of time

長期間にわたって毎日

ⓘ day in, day out の形でも使われる。

例 Working in the fields **day in and day out** is hard on the body.

来る日も来る日も畑で働くのは体にきつい。

058

on your guard

用心して、警戒して

形 very careful and prepared for something difficult or bad to happen

非常に用心し、困難なことまたは悪いことが起こるのに備えて

例 You must always be **on your guard** when in the wilderness.

大自然の中にいるときは、常に注意していなければならない。

059

in the course of time

やがて、そのうち

副 when some or enough time has passed

ある程度または十分な時間が経過したとき

≒ eventually

例 Pippy will get used to her new school **in the course of time**.

ピッピーは、そのうち新しい学校に慣れるだろう。

060

stand on your own feet

自立する

動 to be independent and take care of yourself without any help

独立し、一切助けを借りずに自分のことを自分でやる

ⓘ feet の前に two を入れることもある。

例 His parents helped him out financially until he was able to **stand on his own feet**.

彼が自立できるまで、両親が経済的に援助してくれた。

□□□ 061

to the day

ちょうど、1日もたがわず

副 used to say something happened at the exact same time in the past

過去のまったく同じ時に何かが起こったと述べるのに使われる

ⓘ to the minute（1分もたがわず）という表現もある。

例 It's been four years **to the day** since her grandfather died.

彼女の祖父が亡くなってから今日でちょうど4年になる。

□□□ 062

year after year

来る年も来る年も

副 every year for many years

何年もにわたって毎年

≒ year in, year out

例 **Year after year**, more and more animals are added to the endangered species list.

年々、絶滅危惧種のリストに追加される動物が増えている。

□□□ 063

when it comes to

〜のことになると

前 when you are dealing with something

何かを論じるときには

例 **When it comes to** Marge, you have to speak very loudly for her to be able to hear you.

マージについて言うと、かなり大きな声で話さないとこちらの声が聞こえないんです。

□□□ 064

if anything

むしろ

副 used to say something that disagrees with something else that has been said

すでに述べられたほかの何かと一致しない何かを述べるのに使われる

例 **If anything**, this gives me even more reason to take away your keys to the car.

むしろ、これであなたから車の鍵を取り上げておく理由がさらに増えた。

064句

章末ボキャブラリーチェック

次の語義が表す英熟語を答えてください。

語義	解答	連番
❶ used to introduce extra information and provide emphasis	not to mention	026
❷ still remaining before something happens	to go	052
❸ no longer useful or effective	out of date	002
❹ used to say something has to be done no matter how difficult it may be	at any cost	001
❺ used to say something generally	on the whole	034
❻ at a time or place that is suitable for someone	at someone's convenience	051
❼ used to give more specific information about someone or something just mentioned	that is (to say)	003
❽ modern or fashionable	up to date	023
❾ to watch someone or something carefully and with a lot of interest	be all eyes	036
❿ in spite of something	for all	044
⓫ (of a food order) to be taken away from the restaurant and eaten somewhere else	to go	052
⓬ as much as you want	to your heart's content	055
⓭ to succeed in getting someone to understand what you are saying	make yourself understood	049
⓮ used to say something else could have been done to achieve the same result	may as well do	030
⓯ to be or put yourself in a situation where something bad could happen	run the risk of doing	038
⓰ used to say you are willing to do something	only too	043
⓱ showing thanks to someone or paying them for something they have done	in return for	022
⓲ still needing to be done or dealt with in order to be finished	to go	052

語義	解答	連番
⓳ used to say the opposite of what was previously said is true	on the contrary	033
⓴ sometimes, but not regularly	from time to time	047
㉑ to stop resisting someone or something and agree to do what you do not want to do	give way to	016
㉒ to do what you want regardless of what someone else has said	go your own way	005
㉓ used to say something happened at the exact same time in the past	to the day	061
㉔ to not properly notice or appreciate someone or something	take it for granted that	040
㉕ when some or enough time has passed	in the course of time	059
㉖ made or done by someone	on the part of	024
㉗ to stop something from continuing because it is not good	put an end to	035
㉘ used to say you wish that the situation was different	only too	043
㉙ used to talk about a situation in which something is far away from you in space or time	at a distance	018
㉚ forced to stay in a container in an amount that will make it escape the container with force when opened	under pressure	012
㉛ used to emphasize what you are saying is obvious	needless to say	050
㉜ used to describe being in the same place as another person	in the presence of	017
㉝ after thinking about something	in light of	009
㉞ used to give information that affects something previously mentioned	that is (to say)	003
㉟ used to emphasize you are saying something in an unusual or funny way	so to speak	053
㊱ to go to where you are supposed to be	take your place	006
㊲ used to introduce an additional fact after others have already been mentioned	to say nothing of	054

語義	解答	連番
❸ at some point in the future	one of these days	020
❸ used to tell someone they should do something since there is no reason not to	may as well *do*	030
❹ very careful and prepared for something difficult or bad to happen	on your guard	058
❹ used to say something is done many times	over and over (again)	042
❹ to become known to other people	come to light	025
❹ to be replaced by something	give way to	016
❹ in no way	by no means	008
❹ to imagine yourself in another person's situation	put yourself in *someone's* shoes	037
❹ if something happens	in case of	004
❹ used to say a person is actually at a place	in person	031
❹ to be independent and take care of yourself without any help	stand on your own feet	060
❹ used to politely ask whether something is true	by any chance	046
❺ being forced or urged to do something	under pressure	012
❺ in a way that does damage to someone or something	at the expense of	056
❺ without needing to pay any money	free of charge	029
❺ used to say that something is not important or interesting to you or someone else	for all	044
❺ used to emphasize just how large a number is	as many as	015
❺ used to add more information to what has already been said	in addition to	014
❺ so that something can happen or be done	in order that	041
❺ used to say something that disagrees with something else that has been said	if anything	064
❺ no longer recent and potentially incorrect	out of date	002
❺ to begin holding someone or something	take hold of	021

語義	解答	連番
⑥ to use something unfairly to get what you want	take advantage of	045
⑥ no longer legally acceptable	out of date	002
⑥ given because of something that has been given to you	in exchange for	028
⑥ used to say that you do not know much about something	for all I know	013
⑥ because of something	in light of	009
⑥ to let someone or something be or go first	give way to	016
⑥ for a short period of time that is not permanent	for the time being	032
⑥ instead of what usually is done or happens	for a change	027
⑥ to accept your status in society	take your place	006
⑥ to control your anger and stay calm	keep your temper	011
⑦ in the near future	in the short run	010
⑦ to treat someone unfairly to get what you want	take advantage of	045
⑦ every day for a long period of time	day in and day out	057
⑦ including all the most recent information	up to date	023
⑦ so quickly that it is surprising	in less than no time	007
⑦ every year for many years	year after year	062
⑦ uncertain and undecided	up in the air	019
⑦ when you are dealing with something	when it comes to	063
⑦ to use a situation to do or get what you want	take advantage of	045
⑦ used to start explaining in what way something is true	in that	048
⑧ to look for and point out problems in someone or something, especially unfairly and repeatedly	find fault with	039

TURN OUT (→331)

turn は「向きを変える、回る」「〜を回す」という意味の動詞、out は「外に、出て」「消えて」という意味の副詞で、組み合わさって「回転して何かが出てくる」イメージです。そこから、結果が出てくる、人出がある、製

品などが製造される、といった意味が出てきます。一方、ダイヤルなどを「回して」電灯などを「消す」という意味も表します。

① 結局〔〜と〕なる、〔〜と〕判明する

She was very pleased with how her cake **turned out**.

（彼女はケーキの出来栄えにとても満足していた。）

② （集まりなどに）繰り出す、出かける

Despite the weather, hundreds of fans **turned out** for the game.

（この天気にもかかわらず、何百人ものファンが試合を訪れた。）

③ 〈電灯など〉を消す、〜のスイッチを切る

You forgot to **turn out** the light when you went to bed last night.

（ゆうべ寝るときに電気を消すのを忘れていたよ。）

④ 〜を作り出す、生産する

The band **turns out** a new album almost every year.

（このバンドはほとんど毎年、新しいアルバムを出している。）

Stage 2

A journey of a thousand miles begins with a single step.
千里の道も一歩から。

□ □ □ 065

be up to

〜を企てている

動 ① to do something with bad intentions

悪意を持って何かをする

例 We know you**'re up to** something.

私たちはあなたが何か企んで いるのを知っています。

〜次第だ、
〜に委ねられている

② to say someone can decide something

誰かが何かを決めることが できると述べる

例 It**'s up to** you to decide where we go for dinner.

私たちがどこへ夕食に行くか決 めるのはあなたです。

〜に責任がある

③ to say something is the responsibility of someone

何かが誰かの責任であると 述べる

例 It **is up to** you to make sure everyone is properly taking their lunch break.

みんながきちんと昼休みを取 れるようにするのはあなたの 責任です。

□ □ □ 066

gain time

時間稼ぎをする

動 to delay something so that you have more time before you make a decision, deal with a problem, etc.

決断を下したり、問題に対 処したりする前に、より多く の時間を持てるように何か を遅らせる

≒ buy yourself time

⇔ lose time

例 She asked to use the restroom, trying to **gain time** to think.

彼女は考えるための時間稼ぎ をしようとして、トイレに行かせ てほしいと頼んだ。

□□□ 067

be given to

～しがちだ

動 to have a tendency to do something even though you should not

すべきではないのに、何かをする傾向がある

例 Cleo had never **been given to** complaining about her life.

クレオは、自分の生活に不満をこぼしがちになったことは一度もなかった。

□□□ 068

make light of

～を軽んじる、ないがしろにする

動 to joke about something or act like it is not serious when it is actually important

何かが本当は重要なのに、それについて冗談を言ったり、それが深刻でないかのように振る舞ったりする

⇔ make much of

例 You shouldn't **make light of** your high school graduation, since it will only happen once.

高校の卒業式は一度しかないのだから、軽んじないほうがよい。

□□□ 069

make a difference

重要である

動 ① to have an important effect on someone or something

誰かまたは何かに重要な影響を与える

例 All of your support really **made a difference** in my life.

あなたがしてくれた支援のすべては、私の人生にとても大きな意味があった。

(よい)影響を与える、状況を改善する

② to make a situation better

状況をよりよくする

069句

例 Help **make a difference** by donating today.

本日ご寄付いただくことで、状況の改善にお力添えください。

□□□ 070

turn a deaf ear to

～に聞く耳を持たない

動 to ignore or be unwilling to listen to someone or something

誰かまたは何かを無視する、あるいはその話を聞きたがらない

例 It's like the government has **turned a deaf ear to** the problems of the people.

政府は、国民が抱える問題に聞く耳を持たなくなったようだ。

□□□ 071

take into account

～を考慮に入れる

動 to consider certain information before making a decision or judgment about something

何かについて決定または判断をする前に、特定の情報を検討する

≒ consider

ⓘ 〈take 事物 into account〉のほか、〈take account of 事物〉の形でも使われる。

例 You should have **taken into account** how much we would be walking when you got dressed this morning.

今朝服を着るとき、私たちがどのくらい歩くことになるか考慮に入れるべきだったんですよ。

□□□ 072

at length

ついに、ようやく

副 ① after a long time

長い時間の後で

≒ at last, finally

例 "You're wrong," she said **at length**.

「あなたは間違っています」と、彼女はようやく言った。

長々と、詳細に

② for a long time and with a lot of detail

長い時間をかけて、詳細に

例 Roberto talked **at length** about his trip to the Netherlands.

ロベルトはオランダ旅行について長々と話した。

□□□ 073

let alone

~は言うまでもなく、
まして~なんて

前 used to emphasize that since what was already said is not true or possible, what is said afterward cannot be either

すでに述べたことが真実でも可能でもないので、後に述べることも真実でも可能でもあり得ないということを強調するのに使われる

例 You don't even know how to ride a bicycle, **let alone** drive a car.

あなたは車の運転はおろか、自転車の乗り方さえ知らない。

~を放っておく

動 to stop touching or changing something

何かに触れたり、変化させたりするをやめる

≒ leave alone

例 You need to learn to **let** your sister **alone** when she's grumpy.

妹さんが不機嫌なときは、放っておけるようになりなさい。

□□□ 074

come to terms with

〈人〉と折り合いがつく、
合意に至る

動 ① to reach an agreement with someone

誰かと合意に達する

例 The two teams were eventually forced to **come to terms with** each other.

2つのチームは、最終的に互いに折り合いをつけるしかなかった。

~を受け入れる、
甘受する

② to learn how to accept something that is unpleasant or painful

不快なことや苦痛なことの受け入れ方を身につける

074句

例 It took a long time for her to **come to terms with** her diagnosis.

彼女が自分の診断を受け入れるには長い時間がかかった。

☐☐☐ **075**

in private

内密に

副 without other people present

ほかの人がいないところで

≒ privately

例 What you do **in private** is your business.

プライベートですることはあなたの自由です。

☐☐☐ **076**

make believe

〜のふりをする

動 to pretend something is true when it is not

何かが真実ではないのに、真実であるふりをする

例 As a child, she used to **make believe** that she was a chef with her own bakery.

子どもの頃、彼女は自分のパン屋を持つシェフになったつもりでいた。

☐☐☐ **077**

prior to

〜より前に

前 before something else

ほかの何かの前に

例 **Prior to** the invention of GPS, people had to read maps to get around unfamiliar places.

GPS が発明される前は、人々はなじみのない場所を移動するのに地図を読まなければならなかった。

☐☐☐ **078**

due to

**〜のために、
〜が理由で**

前 because of or caused by someone or something

誰かまたは何かのせいで、あるいはそれによって引き起こされた

例 The highway has been closed **due to** heavy rain.

大雨のため、その幹線道路は通行止めになっている。

□□□ **079**

nothing less than

〜にほかならない、
まさしく〜

副 ① used to emphasize the greatness of something

何かのすごさを強調するの
に使われる

例 The work you have done is **nothing less than** extraordinary.

あなたが成し遂げた仕事は、ま
さしく途方もないことだ。

ただ〜だけ

② used to say that something or someone is the least that can be accepted

何かまたは誰かが、受け入
れられ得る最低限だと述べ
るのに使われる

例 The boss will accept **nothing less than** top quality proposals.

上司は、最高レベルの提案し
か受け入れないだろう。

□□□ **080**

as of

〈特定の日付〉から、
〜以後

前 ① from a specific date

特定の日付から

≒ as from

例 **As of** January 15th, we will no longer offer plastic bags for free with purchases.

1月15日より、お買い上げの際
のレジ袋の無料配布を終了さ
せていただきます。

〈特定の日付〉時点で

② on a specific date

特定の日に

例 **As of** June 3rd, there had not even been 100 applications for the new category of visa.

6月3日時点で、新しいカテゴ
リーのビザの申請は100件も
なかった。

080句

□□□ **081**

in the long run

長い目で見れば、
結局は

副 used when talking about something that will happen later or when something is finished

後で起こることについて話すとき、または何かが終わったときに使われる

≒ in the long term

⇔ in the short run

例 Moving to the countryside will be better for your health **in the long run**.

田舎に引っ越したほうが、長い目で見ればあなたの健康によいだろう。

□□□ **082**

beyond words

言葉では言い表せない
（ほど）

形 in a way that cannot be said using words

言葉では言い表せない方法で

例 My disappointment in your actions is **beyond words**.

あなたの行為に対する失望は、言葉になりません。

□□□ **083**

on your way

進行中で、近づいていて

形 ① happening or arriving soon

間もなく起きる、または到着する

≒ in progress

例 There is a box of goodies **on its way** to you.

おいしいものの入った箱をお手元にお届け中です。

（〜に向かう）途中で

② going from one place to another

ある場所から別の場所へ移動している

例 They are **on their way** to visit the Grand Canyon.

彼らは、グランドキャニオンを訪れる途中だ。

□□□ 084

still less

まして〜なんてとんでも
ない

前 used to say that something is even less
true than what you have already said

何かが、すでに言ったことよ
りもさらに真実でないという
ことを述べるのに使われる

≒ much less

ⓘ 主にイギリス英語。

例 She's too nervous to even talk to you, **still less** to go
dancing.

彼女は緊張しすぎて君と話すこ
とさえできないし、ましてや踊り
に行くなんてとんでもないよ。

□□□ 085

take a risk

危険を冒す

動 to do something with the possibility of a
bad result

悪い結果となる可能性があ
る中で何かをする

例 We **took a risk** coming to pick you up in the middle of
a snowstorm.

私たちは吹雪の中、危険を冒し
てあなたを迎えにきました。

□□□ 086

to say the least

控え目に言っても

to used to emphasize something that has
been said

述べられたことを強調する
のに使われる

例 Her way of speaking was unusual, **to say the least**.

彼女の話し方は、控え目に言っ
てもふつうではなかった。

□□□ 087

as good as

〜も同然で

形 almost or nearly

ほとんど、またはもう少しで

087句

例 When she heard the diagnosis, she thought she was
as good as dead, but she survived in the end.

彼女は、診断結果を聞いたとき
は死んだも同然だと思ったが、
結局は生き延びた。

□□□ **088**

at *someone's* disposal

〈人〉が自由に使える

形 available for someone to use

誰かが利用できる

例 Even with all these tools **at my disposal**, I still wasn't able to design the car of my dreams.

これだけの道具が自由に使えても、私は夢の車を設計できなかった。

□□□ **089**

what is more

そのうえ、さらに

副 used to add more information and emphasize what you are saying

より多くの情報を追加し、自分が言っていることを強調するのに使われる

≒ furthermore

例 You know you're wrong, and **what's more**, you don't care.

あなたは自分が間違っているとわかっていて、しかもそれを気にしない。

□□□ **090**

What for?

なぜ、何のために

構 used to ask the reason or purpose for something

何かの理由や目的を尋ねるのに使われる

例 I bought this yarn at the fabric store. — **What for?**

生地屋でこの糸を買ったんだ――何のために?

□□□ **091**

have your (own) way

我を通す、
したいようにする

動 to get or do what you want after someone has tried to stop you

誰かに止められそうになった後、望むものを手に入れる、あるいは望むことをする

≒ get your (own) way

例 If you think you're going to **have your own way** just because you cried, you're mistaken.

泣いたからって自分の思いどおりになると思ったら、大間違いだ。

□□□ 092

not to say

～とは言わないまでも

to used to say something in a stronger way

より強い言い方で何かを述べるのに使われる

ⓘ 主にイギリス英語。

例 Your presentation is lacking in style, **not to say** incomplete.

あなたのプレゼンは、不完全とは言わないまでも、華々しさが足りない。

□□□ 093

for good

永遠に

副 finally and without the possibility of change in the future

最終的に、また将来変化する可能性もなく

≒ for good and all

例 It appears that she has left **for good** this time.

彼女は今度は永遠に戻ってこないようだ。

□□□ 094

come of age

成人する

動 ① to reach the age when you are considered an adult legally

法的に成人と見なされる年齢に達する

例 Her grandparents **came of age** in a time very different from now.

彼女の祖父母は、今とはまるで違う時代に成人した。

十分に発達する

② to become accepted and respected by most people after developing for a period of time

一定期間発展した後、ほとんどの人に受け入れられ、尊重されるようになる

094句

例 During this period, jazz music **came of age** as a legitimate music style.

この時期に、ジャズは正統な音楽スタイルとして確立された。

□□□ **095**

but for

～がなければ

前 ① used to say something would have happened if something or someone else had not done something

ほかの何かまたは誰かが何かをしなかったとしたら、何かが起こったであろうと述べるのに使われる

≒ without

例 We might have actually won the game **but for** your poor playing tonight.

君のお粗末なプレイがなければ、実は私たちは今夜の試合に勝てたかもしれない。

～を別にすれば

② except for someone or something

誰かまたは何かを除いて

例 All was quiet **but for** the sound of the wind blowing through the trees.

木々の間を吹き抜ける風の音を別にすれば、すべてが静かだった。

□□□ **096**

in connection with

～に関連して

前 for reasons related to someone or something

誰かまたは何かに関連する理由で

ⓘ 特にジャーナリズムで使われる。

例 Police are searching for the man **in connection with** the string of robberies that happened last week.

先週起きた一連の強盗事件に関連して、警察はその男を捜索している。

□□□ **097**

with regard to

～に関して

前 relating to someone or something

誰かまたは何かに関連する

≒ as to, in respect of, with respect to

例 **With regard to** your new position, we ask that you keep it to yourself for now.

あなたの新しい職位に関しては、今のところ内密にしておいてください。

□□□ 098

no doubt

確かに、間違いなく

副 ① used to say you think what you are saying is certainly true

自分の言っていることは確実に本当だと思うと述べるのに使われる

≒ doubtless, unquestionably

例 **No doubt** she will win the competition.

彼女は間違いなく大会で優勝すると思う。

たぶん、おそらく

② used to say you think something is likely

何かがあり得ると思うと述べるのに使われる

例 **No doubt** you have a specific way you want to do things.

たぶんあなたにはあなたのやり方というものがあるんだろう。

□□□ 099

vice versa

逆も同じだ

副 used to say the opposite of what you just said is also true

今言ったのと逆のことも真実であると述べるときに使われる

例 We can give Ash the blue train and Quinn the red one, or **vice versa**.

アッシュには青い電車、クインには赤い電車をあげよう。あるいは、逆でもいいけど。

□□□ 100

in theory

理論上は

副 used to say something should be true, but may actually be wrong

真実であるはずの何かが、実際には間違っているかもしれないと述べるのに使われる

100句

⇔ in practice

例 **In theory**, the new tax system is supposed to benefit small business owners, but that isn't the case at all.

理論上は、新しい税制度は中小企業の経営者に恩恵があるはずだが、実際にはまるでそうなっていない。

□□□ 101

for the moment

差し当たり、当面は

副 used to say something is true now, but might change in the future

今は正しいが、将来的には変わるかもしれないと述べるのに使われる

≒ for the present

例 **For the moment** it would be better if you didn't give your opinion so freely.

当面は、そんなに自由に意見を言わないほうがいいですよ。

□□□ 102

as a whole

全体として

副 used to say all parts of something are considered to be one thing

何かのすべての部分が一つのものであると見なされると述べるのに使われる

例 The nation **as a whole** will benefit from the new infrastructure bill.

インフラに関する新たな法案によって国全体が恩恵を被ることになるだろう。

□□□ 103

at a glance

一目で、一見して

副 with only a quick look

ぱっと見ただけで

≒ immediately

例 An expert can tell **at a glance** whether a painting is authentic or not.

専門家は絵が本物かどうかを一目で見分けることができる。

□□□ 104

by virtue of

～によって、
～のおかげで

前 by means of or as a result of something

何かを手段として、または何かの結果として

例 He became a Canadian citizen **by virtue of** being born in the country.

彼はカナダで生まれたことにより、カナダ国民になった。

□□□ 105

hand in hand

手をつないで、
手に手を取って

副 ① holding another person's hand

ほかの人の手を握って

例 The couple walked **hand in hand** down the
boardwalk.

そのカップルは手をつないで
遊歩道を歩いた。

相伴って

**② used to say some people or things are
very closely connected or related**

ある人々やものが非常に密
接につながっている、また
は関連していると述べるの
に使われる

例 Sometimes mental health issues and artistic genius go
hand in hand.

時に、メンタルヘルスの問題と
芸術的な才能は密接に関連し
ている。

□□□ 106

in effect

〈法律などが〉施行され
て、効力のある

形 ① active or being used

有効で、または使われて

例 There are many antiquated laws still **in effect** in many
states.

多くの州には、未だに施行され
ている時代遅れの法律がたく
さんある。

事実上は

**② used when you are saying what you
think are the real facts of a situation**

ある状況について本当の事
実だと思うことを述べてい
るときに使われる

≒ effectively

106句

例 **In effect**, you are creating a discriminatory
environment.

事実上、あなたは差別的な環
境を作り出していることになり
ます。

□□□ **107**

in comparison with

~と比べて

前 when compared with someone or something

誰かまたは何かと比較すると

≒ by comparison with

例 **In comparison with** his design, yours is very refreshing.

彼のデザインに比べて、あなたのデザインはとてもさわやかです。

□□□ **108**

in no time

あっという間に

副 very soon or very quickly

すぐに、またはとても早く

例 You'll get better **in no time**!

すぐによくなりますよ!

□□□ **109**

in practice

実際は、実際上は

副 used to say what really happens versus what should happen

起こるはずのことと対比して、実際に起こることを述べるのに使われる

≒ in reality

⇔ in theory

例 **In practice**, women are often still expected to stay home while their husbands go to work.

実際には、夫が働いている間、女性は家にいるのをいまだに期待されることが多い。

□□□ **110**

in view of

~を考慮して、
~から考えて

前 used to introduce the reason for something

何かの理由を導入するのに使われる

例 **In view of** what happened last night, we feel it is best to postpone the banquet.

昨夜起こったことを考えると、宴会は延期するのがベストだという感じがする。

□□□ 111

more often than not

たいてい、通例

副 happening more than half the time

半分以上の頻度で起きて

≒ usually, as often as not

例 **More often than not**, there are genuine reasons why a child is misbehaving.

子どもが悪さをするのにはたいてい、本当の理由がある。

□□□ 112

give up for lost

助からない［死んだ］ものとあきらめる

動 to think someone is dead and stop trying to find them

誰かが死んだものと考え、見つけようとするのをやめる

≒ give up for dead

ⓘ 〈give 人 up for lost〉の形で使われる。

例 After months of searching, the police **gave** her **up for lost**.

何か月も捜索したのち、警察は彼女を助からないものとあきらめた。

□□□ 113

at rest

止まって、静止して

形 ① not moving

動いていない

例 When **at rest**, the insect is indistinguishable from a stick.

その虫は、止まっていると小枝と見分けがつかない。

死んで、永眠して

② dead and therefore free from pain and problems

死んだ結果、痛みや問題から解放されて

113句

例 Her grandfather lies **at rest** in the local cemetery.

彼女の祖父は地元の墓地に眠っている。

□□□ **114**

go so far as to *do*

~しさえする、~までする

動 to be willing to or do something extreme when dealing with something

何かに取り組むときに極端なことをすることをいとわない、またはする

例 I can't believe she would **go so far as to** lie to get into the program.

彼女がうそをついてまでそのプログラムに参加するなんて、私には信じられない。

□□□ **115**

to the full

十分に

副 in the most complete way possible

可能な限り完全な仕方で

ⓘ イギリス英語。アメリカ英語では to the fullest とも言う。

例 Everyone at the concert enjoyed it **to the full**.

そのコンサートに参加した全員が十分に楽しんだ。

□□□ **116**

to the point

適切な、要を得た

形 dealing with the important thing without adding anything unnecessary

不要なものを加えずに、重要なことに対処している

例 The marketing manager is always brief and **to the point** with her explanations.

マーケティング部長はいつも、説明が簡潔で要を得ている。

□□□ **117**

take note of

~に注意を払う

動 to pay attention to something and remember it

何かに注意を払い、それを覚える

例 Be sure to **take note of** the weight limits for baggage.

手荷物の重量制限にご注意ください。

□□□ 118

talking of

～と言えば

前 used to say more about something that has already been mentioned

すでに言及されていることについて、さらに多くのことを述べるのに使われる

≒ talking about

ⓘ 主にイギリス英語。

例 **Talking of** Mr. Walker, how is he doing these days?

ウォーカーさんと言えば、彼は最近どうしていますか。

□□□ 119

think highly of

～を高く評価する

動 to have a very good opinion of someone or something

誰かまたは何かについてとても高く評価する

≒ think a lot of

例 Your music teacher told me she **thinks** very **highly of** you.

音楽の先生は、あなたのことをとても高く評価していると言っていました。

□□□ 120

in turn

順に、その次に

副 ① following one after the other in a specific order

特定の順序で次々と続いて

例 They had to describe their experiences to the counselor **in turn**.

彼らは、自分の経験を順番にカウンセラーに話さなければならなかった。

その結果

120句

② as a result of something

何かの結果として

例 Taxes were increased, and, **in turn**, more people struggled to buy food than before.

税金が上がり、その結果、以前より食べ物を買うのに苦労する人が増えた。

□□□ **121**

out of fashion

流行遅れで

形 no longer popular or fashionable

もはや人気がなくなった、または流行しなくなった

⇔ in fashion

例 Velvet clothes have been **out of fashion** for ages.

ベルベットの服は、ずっと前から流行遅れだ。

□□□ **122**

in a way

ある点では、ある程度は

副 when considered in a particular manner

特定の仕方で考慮されると

ⓘ in one way, in some ways の形でも使われる。

例 **In a way**, forcing this through to production was one of our biggest mistakes.

ある意味、これを無理に生産まで推し進めてしまったのは、私たちの最大の誤りの1つだった。

□□□ **123**

keep pace with

〜に（遅れずに）ついていく

動 to change or move as fast as something or someone else

ほかの何かまたは誰かと同じ速さで変化する、あるいは移動する

≒ keep up with

例 Julie is able to **keep pace with** the older kids despite her smaller size.

ジュリーは、体格が小さいにもかかわらず、年上の子どもたちについていくことができる。

□□□ **124**

to be sure

確かに

副 used to admit something is true

何かが真実であることを認めるのに使われる

例 **To be sure**, making your stay as enjoyable as possible is our top priority.

確かに、お客さまのご宿泊をできるだけ楽しいものにすることが、私たちの最優先事項です。

□□□ **125**

at will

思いのままに、自由に

副 whenever you want and wherever you like

好きなときに、好きなところで

例 All staff are encouraged to take their breaks **at will**.

スタッフは皆、自由に休憩を取ってください。

□□□ **126**

take turns

交代で〜する

動 doing or sharing something one after the other

交代で何かをする、または何かを共有する

例 **Take turns** with your sister when you play that game.

そのゲームをするときはお姉ちゃんと交代でしてね。

□□□ **127**

get the better of

〜に勝つ、
〜を打ち負かす

動 ① to defeat someone or something by being clever

誰かまたは何かを巧みに打ち負かす

例 He finally **got the better of** his chess opponent.

彼はついにチェスの対戦相手に勝った。

（感情などが）〜を圧倒する

② to cause someone to behave differently from how they should or would like to

誰かに、とるべきあるいはとりたい態度とは違う態度をとらせる

127句

例 She let her emotions **get the better of** her and sent her boss a very rude email.

彼女は感情に流され、上司にとても失礼なメールを送ってしまった。

章末ボキャブラリーチェック

次の語義が表す英熟語を答えてください。

語義	解答	連番
❶ finally and without the possibility of change in the future	for good	093
❷ by means of or as a result of something	by virtue of	104
❸ used when you are saying what you think are the real facts of a situation	in effect	106
❹ when considered in a particular manner	in a way	122
❺ used to say what really happens versus what should happen	in practice	109
❻ holding another person's hand	hand in hand	105
❼ relating to someone or something	with regard to	097
❽ to change or move as fast as something or someone else	keep pace with	123
❾ for reasons related to someone or something	in connection with	096
❿ for a long time and with a lot of detail	at length	072
⓫ to reach the age when you are considered an adult legally	come of age	094
⓬ available for someone to use	at someone's disposal	088
⓭ to ignore or be unwilling to listen to someone or something	turn a deaf ear to	070
⓮ used to emphasize the greatness of something	nothing less than	079
⓯ dead and therefore free from pain and problems	at rest	113
⓰ used to emphasize something that has been said	to say the least	086
⓱ very soon or very quickly	in no time	108
⓲ to pretend something is true when it is not	make believe	076
⓳ whenever you want and wherever you like	at will	125
⓴ used to say something in a stronger way	not to say	092

語義	解答	連番
❷❶ used to add more information and emphasize what you are saying	w h a t i s m o r e	089
❷❷ to learn how to accept something that is unpleasant or painful	c o m e t o t e r m s w i t h	074
❷❸ used when talking about something that will happen later or when something is finished	i n t h e l o n g r u n	081
❷❹ to say someone can decide something	b e u p t o	065
❷❺ used to admit something is true	t o b e s u r e	124
❷❻ used to say the opposite of what you just said is also true	v i c e v e r s a	099
❷❼ used to ask the reason or purpose for something	W h a t f o r ?	090
❷❽ not moving	a t r e s t	113
❷❾ to have an important effect on someone or something	m a k e a d i f f e r e n c e	069
❸❶ used to say all parts of something are considered to be one thing	a s a w h o l e	102
❸❶ used to say that something is even less true than what you have already said	s t i l l l e s s	084
❸❷ before something else	p r i o r t o	077
❸❸ used to say you think something is likely	n o d o u b t	098
❸❹ to have a very good opinion of someone or something	t h i n k h i g h l y o f	119
❸❺ following one after the other in a specific order	i n t u r n	120
❸❻ to pay attention to something and remember it	t a k e n o t e o f	117
❸❼ as a result of something	i n t u r n	120
❸❽ to say something is the responsibility of someone	b e u p t o	065
❸❾ to reach an agreement with someone	c o m e t o t e r m s w i t h	074
❹❶ to have a tendency to do something even though you should not	b e g i v e n t o	067
❹❶ used to say more about something that has already been mentioned	t a l k i n g o f	118

❷ to be willing to or do something extreme when dealing with something — <u>go so far as to do</u> — 114

❸ to make a situation better — <u>make a difference</u> — 069

❹ to joke about something or act like it is not serious when it is actually important — <u>make light of</u> — 068

❺ almost or nearly — <u>as good as</u> — 087

❻ in a way that cannot be said using words — <u>beyond words</u> — 082

❼ to think someone is dead and stop trying to find them — <u>give up for lost</u> — 112

❽ to cause someone to behave differently from how they should or would like to — <u>get the better of</u> — 127

❾ after a long time — <u>at length</u> — 072

❺ to stop touching or changing something — <u>let alone</u> — 073

❺ happening or arriving soon — <u>on your way</u> — 083

❺ no longer popular or fashionable — <u>out of fashion</u> — 121

❺ to do something with the possibility of a bad result — <u>take a risk</u> — 085

❺ to get or do what you want after someone has tried to stop you — <u>have your (own) way</u> — 091

❺ to defeat someone or something by being clever — <u>get the better of</u> — 127

❺ used to say that something or someone is the least that can be accepted — <u>nothing less than</u> — 079

❺ except for someone or something — <u>but for</u> — 095

❺ to do something with bad intentions — <u>be up to</u> — 065

❺ used to say something should be true, but may actually be wrong — <u>in theory</u> — 100

❻ used to say something would have happened if something or someone else had not done something — <u>but for</u> — 095

❻ used to say some people or things are very closely connected or related — <u>hand in hand</u> — 105

❻ used to say you think what you are saying is certainly true — <u>no doubt</u> — 098

語義	解答	連番
❸ when compared with someone or something	in comparison with	107
❹ from a specific date	as of	080
❺ without other people present	in private	075
❻ doing or sharing something one after the other	take turns	126
❼ with only a quick look	at a glance	103
❽ active or being used	in effect	106
❾ dealing with the important thing without adding anything unnecessary	to the point	116
❼⓪ to consider certain information before making a decision or judgment about something	take into account	071
❼❶ to delay something so that you have more time before you make a decision, deal with a problem, etc.	gain time	066
❼❷ used to introduce the reason for something	in view of	110
❼❸ on a specific date	as of	080
❼❹ in the most complete way possible	to the full	115
❼❺ used to say something is true now, but might change in the future	for the moment	101
❼❻ happening more than half the time	more often than not	111
❼❼ used to emphasize that since what was already said is not true or possible, what is said afterward cannot be either	let alone	073
❼❽ to become accepted and respected by most people after developing for a period of time	come of age	094
❼❾ because of or caused by someone or something	due to	078
❽⓪ going from one place to another	on your way	083

GET INTO (→335)

getは「〜を得る」「〜になる」が基本的な意味の動詞ですが、「移動する、着く」という意味もあります。intoは「〜の中に」という意味の前置詞で、get intoと組み合わせると、「〜の中に入る、入り込む」という

イメージの句動詞になります。文字どおり「〜の中に入る」という意味のほか、「〈よくない事柄〉に巻き込まれる」、「服に入り込む」→「〜を（なんとか）身に着ける、着る」、「〜に興味を持つ、はまる」といった意味が出てきます。

①〜の中に入る

I lost my keys, and now I can't **get into** my apartment.
（私は鍵をなくしてしまい、今アパートに入れないんです。）

②〈よくない事柄〉に巻き込まれる

We'll **get into** trouble if we use Dad's computer.
（お父さんのコンピュータを使ったら面倒なことになるよ。）

③〜を（なんとか）身に着ける、着る

I wonder if I'd still be able to **get into** my wedding dress.
（私のウエディングドレス、まだ入るかなあ。）

④〜に興味を持つ、はまる

Recently I've been **getting into** fishing.
（最近、釣りにはまっている。）

Stage 3

Practice makes perfect.
継続は力なり。

□□□ **128**

on end

直立して

副 ① in an upright position

直立した体勢で

例 Stand the box **on end** so it takes up less space.

箱があまり場所を取らないように、直立させて置こう。

続けて

② for the length of time specified and without stopping

明示された時間の間、止まることなく

≒ continuously, in a row

例 Her father used to disappear for weeks **on end** when she was a child.

彼女が幼い頃、父親はよく何週間も行方知れずになった。

□□□ **129**

under way

（乗り物などが）動き始めて

形 ① having started to move or go somewhere

動き始めて、あるいはどこかに向かい始めて

ⓘ underwayともつづる。

例 We apologize for the delay. The train should be **under way** again shortly.

お待たせし申し訳ございません。電車はまもなく運転を再開します。

進行中で

② having already started

すでに始まっていて

≒ in progress

例 Plans are **under way** for a new stadium for the local baseball team.

地元球団のための新しいスタジアムの計画が進行中だ。

□□□ 130

on behalf of

〈人〉を代表して、
〈人〉の代わりに

前 ① instead of someone

誰かの代わりに

ⓘ on *someone's* behalf の形でも使われる（②③も）。

例 We submit visa applications **on behalf of** our clients.

私たちはお客さまに代わって
ビザの申請を行います。

〜のために、
〜を助けるために

② in order to help someone

誰かを助けるために

例 After the accident, her father set up a donation page **on behalf of** her.

事故後、彼女の父親は彼女を
救済するための寄付のページ
を開設した。

〜のせいで

③ because of someone or for someone

誰かのせいで、あるいは誰
かのために

例 Please don't worry **on behalf of** me.

私のことで心配しないでください。

□□□ 131

look in the eye

〈人〉の目を見る、
直視する

動 to look straight at someone who is also looking at you

自分を見ている人を直視する

ⓘ 〈look 人 in the eye〉の形で使われる。look in the face とも言う。

131句

例 His father taught him to always **look** someone **in the eye** when shaking hands with them.

握手するときは必ず相手の目
を見るようにと、父親は彼に教
えた。

□□□ **132**

well off

恵まれた、うまくいって

形 ① being in a good situation

よい状況にある

例 Given what other people are going through, I think I'm pretty **well off** right now.

ほかの人が経験していることを考えると、私は今かなり恵まれていると思う。

裕福な

② having a lot of money

たくさんのお金を持っている

≒ rich
⇔ badly off

例 He realized her family was **well off** when she invited him to their beach house.

一家のビーチハウスに招待されて、彼は彼女の家族が裕福であることがわかった。

□□□ **133**

as yet

今のところまだ、そのときはまだ

副 until and including the present

現在まで、そして現在を含めて

≒ as of yet

例 We haven't heard from Ms. Burns **as yet**.

私たちはバーンズさんからまだ連絡がない。

□□□ **134**

take a chance

いちかばちかやってみる

動 to do something where there is a chance something could go wrong

うまくいかない可能性がある中で何かをする

例 If you don't **take a chance** now, you might not be able to later.

今いちかばちかやってみなければ、後でやることはできないかもしれませんよ。

□□□ 135

in the way

邪魔になって

形 stopping someone or something from moving or doing something

誰かまたは何かが動いたり、何かをしたりするのを妨げて

ⓘ 誰[何]の邪魔になっているかを明示するin *someone's* [*something's*] wayという言い方もある。

例 The truck is **in the way**, so no other vehicles can pass.

トラックが邪魔で、ほかの車が通れない。

□□□ 136

fall short of

〈基準・期待など〉に達しない、届かない

動 to be less than what was expected or is needed

予想されたもの、または必要とされるものより少ない

例 The budget this year **falls short of** what we expected.

今年の予算は、私たちが予想していたものに達しない。

□□□ 137

at intervals

時間をおいて

副 ① with some time between

間に時間をおいて

例 The train leaves the station **at** five-minute **intervals**.

電車は5分間隔で駅を出発する。

間隔をおいて、所々に

② with some space between

間に間隔をおいて

137句

例 The guards were stationed **at** even **intervals** along the fence.

警備員はフェンス沿いに等間隔に配置されていた。

☐☐☐ **138**

in relation to

~に比べて

前 ① used to show how something you are talking about is compared to another thing

自分が話題にしている何かが別のものとどう比べられるかを示すのに使われる

≒ in comparison to, compared with [to], relative to

例 Dogs are seen as more social **in relation to** cats.

犬は猫に比べて社交的だと考えられている。

~について

② related to something

何かに関連して

≒ in [with] reference to, regarding

例 There is nothing else left to say **in relation to** this matter.

この件に関しては、もう言うことはほかに何もない。

☐☐☐ **139**

on and off

断続的に、ときどき

副 starting and stopping over and over again

起動と停止を何度も繰り返して

≒ off and on

例 Ella has been learning Korean **on and off** for a few months now.

エラは数か月前から韓国語を断続的に勉強している。

☐☐☐ **140**

in any event

いずれにしても

副 used to emphasize that something will definitely happen or be true despite something else

ほかの何かにもかかわらず、何かが確実に起こる、または真実であるということを強調するのに使われる

≒ at all events, in any case, in either event

例 Even if the game is canceled, I'll come over **in any event**.

試合が中止になっても、私はいずれにしても向かいます。

□□□ 141

not in the least

まったく～ない

圓 not at all

まったく～ない

例 She does**n't** appear to be hungry **in the least**.

彼女はお腹が空いているように
はまったく見えない。

□□□ 142

make good

成功する、出世する

動 ① to become successful and rich after being poor

貧しかった後、成功して金持
ちになる

≒ make it good

例 The local newspaper reported on how Ms. Sampson **made good** when she moved to San Francisco.

地元の新聞は、サンプソンさん
がサンフランシスコに移ってか
ら、どうやって成功したかにつ
いて報道した。

（約束などを）果たす

② to do something you have said you would do

自分がすると言ったことを
する

≒ fulfil

ⓘ 〈make good on 事物〉の形で使われることが多い。

例 She'll **make good** on her promise, so don't worry too much about it.

彼女は約束を果たすので、その
ことについてはあまり心配しな
いでください。

〈損害など〉を修復する、
補償する

142句

③ to fix, replace, or pay for something you have done wrong or damaged

自分が間違ったことや破損
したものの修理、交換、ある
いはその支払いをする

ⓘ イギリス英語。〈make 事物 good〉の形で使われる。

例 Harold **made** the computer **good** again after a bit of work.

ハロルドは、少し作業してコン
ピュータを修復した。

□□□ **143**

so much for

〜についてはこれだけ
（にしておく）

形 ① used to show you are done talking about something

何かについて話し終わった
ことを示すのに使われる

例 **So much for** weather. Now let's move on to sports.

以上、お天気でした。次にス
ポーツの話題に移りましょう。

〜なんてそんなもの、
期待外れ

② used to say that something was not useful or did not produce a good result

何かが役に立たなかった、
あるいはよい結果をもたら
さなかったと述べるのに使
われる

例 Well, **so much for** that idea. Let's try Bill's idea now.

そのアイデアはもういいよ。ビ
ルのアイデアを試してみよう。

□□□ **144**

be confronted with

〜に直面している

動 to have to deal with something or someone difficult or threatening

困難な、あるいは脅威にな
る何かまたは誰かに対処し
なければならない

例 When you**'re confronted with** a problem, just think about it sensibly and act accordingly.

問題に直面したときは、分別を
持って考え、それに従って行動
してください。

□□□ **145**

by and large

全体的に見て、概して

副 used when making a general statement

一般論を述べるときに使わ
れる

≒ in general, generally, for the most part

例 **By and large**, our new business has been very successful.

概して、私たちの新しいビジネ
スはとてもうまくいっている。

□□□ **146**

make a point of *doing*

〜するよう心がける、
必ず〜するようにする

動 to do something on purpose, even when it involves extra effort

さらに努力が必要となる場合でも、あえて何かをする

≒ make it a point to *do*

例 Eri always **makes a point of** making coffee for everyone in the office in the morning.

エリはいつも、職場のみんなに朝のコーヒーを淹れることにしている。

□□□ **147**

for short

（名前を）略して

副 in a shorter form

より短い形で

例 His real name is Theodore, but everyone calls him Ted **for short**.

彼の本名はセオドアだが、みんなは略してテッドと呼んでいる。

□□□ **148**

for that matter

それについては（〜も同じだ）

副 used to add to what you have just said

自分が今言ったばかりのことに追加するのに使われる

例 Anna never drinks coffee, or any other caffeinated beverages **for that matter**.

アンナはコーヒーを決して飲まないし、そのほかのカフェイン入りの飲み物についても同じだ。

□□□ **149**

at the mercy of

〜のなすがままで

149句

形 not able to protect yourself from someone or something because they have control

誰かまたは何かの支配下にあり、それらから自分を守ることができない

ⓘ 〈at *someone's* [*something's*] mercy〉の形でも使われる。

例 On their tiny boat, they were **at the mercy of** the weather.

ちっぽけなボートに乗った彼らは天気のなすがままになっていた。

on top of

〜の上に

前 ① on the surface of something

何かの表面に

例 She put the cookies **on top of** the fridge so her children couldn't reach them.

彼女は子どもたちの手が届かないように、クッキーを冷蔵庫の上に置いた。

〜に加えて

② in addition to something

何かに加えて

例 **On top of** being sick, she also has a ton of deadlines.

彼女は体調がよくないうえ、山ほど締め切りも抱えている。

〈事態など〉に精通して、〈仕事など〉をこなして

③ in complete control of something

何かを完全に掌握して

例 Caleb is **on top of** everything and will make sure nothing goes wrong.

カレブはすべてのことを把握し、問題が起こらないように目を光らせている。

〜のすぐそばに

④ very close to someone or something

誰かまたは何かのすぐ近くに

例 The tiger was nearly **on top of** them before they realized it was there.

いつの間にか、トラは彼らのほんのすぐそばまで来ていた。

□□□ 151

to the contrary

それとは逆の

形 showing or saying the opposite

逆のことを示す、または述べる

例 Unless there is evidence **to the contrary**, I always assume people are telling me the truth.

逆のことを示す証拠がない限り、私はいつも人が真実を語っていると決めてかかっている。

□□□ 152

go far

〈人が〉成功する、出世する

動 to be very successful in the future

将来大成功する

例 If you keep making songs this good, you'll **go far** in the music industry.

これだけいい曲を作り続ければ、音楽業界で活躍できますよ。

□□□ 153

keep track of

～の所在[動向など]を追う

動 to pay attention to someone or something and know what they are doing or where they are

誰かまたは何かに注意を払い、何をしているかあるいはどこにいるかを知る

⇔ lose track of

例 It was hard for the nanny to **keep track of** all the kids while they played in the park.

子どもたちが公園で遊んでいる間、ベビーシッターが全員の動きを追うのは大変だった。

□□□ 154

inside out

裏返しに、表裏逆に

副 with the parts that are normally inside on the outside

通常は内側にある部分を外側にして

例 Dee accidentally went to work with her sweater on **inside out**.

ディーは、うっかりセーターを裏返しに着て仕事に出かけた。

154句

□□□ **155**

in terms of

~の点で、~に関して

前 used to show a specific thing that is being talked about

話題になっている特定のものを示すのに使われる

例 **In terms of** performance, you are at the top of the list.

業績に関しては、あなたはトップです。

□□□ **156**

at your earliest convenience

ご都合がつき次第

副 as soon as possible

できるだけ早く

ⓘ 主にビジネス通信文で使う。

例 We ask that you please return these forms **at your earliest convenience**.

ご都合がつき次第、こちらのフォームをご返送くださるようお願いします。

□□□ **157**

as often as not

たいてい、しばしば

副 usually, or in most situations

通常、またはほとんどの状況で

≒ more often than not

例 The buses arrive late **as often as not**, so don't rely on them if you have a tight schedule.

バスは遅れて来ることが多いので、時間に余裕がないときは当てにしないでください。

□□□ **158**

hard up for

~がなくて困っている

形 not having what you want or need

欲しいものや必要なものを持っていない

ⓘ hard upだけで「金欠で」という意味もある。

例 He must be **hard up for** cash if he's selling his boat.

ボートを売るということは、彼は金に困っているに違いない。

□□□ 159

hold your breath

息を止める

動 ① to stop breathing for a short time on purpose

意図的に短時間呼吸を止める

例 My kids play a game where they **hold their breath** whenever the car drives through a tunnel.

うちの子どもたちは、車がトンネルを通るたびに息を止める遊びをする。

期待しない

② used to say that you do not believe that something will happen soon or maybe ever

何かがすぐに起きない、あるいはずっと起きないかもしれないと思うと述べるのに使われる

ⓘ 否定文で使われる。

例 My husband told me he was going to fix the sprinklers, but I'm not **holding my breath**.

夫はスプリンクラーを修理すると言っていたが、私は期待していない。

□□□ 160

make money

金をもうける

動 to earn money from doing something

何かをすることでお金を稼ぐ

例 You could **make money** as a recruiter.

あなたはリクルーターとしてお金を稼ぐこともできる。

□□□ 161

make sense of

～を理解する

161句

動 to understand something that is complicated

複雑な何かを理解する

例 It took him a while, but he finally **made sense of** the math problem he was working on.

しばらく時間がかかったが、彼はついに取り組んでいた数学の問題を理解した。

□□□ **162**

drive home

~をよく理解させる

動 to make someone understand something by saying it aggressively

強く言うことによって、誰かに何かを理解させる

例 He showed a picture of some fish killed by the pollution to really **drive** the point **home**.

彼は言わんとすることをよく理解してもらおうと、汚染によって死んだ魚の写真を見せた。

□□□ **163**

far and wide

広範囲に

副 over a large area

広い範囲にわたって

例 People came from **far and wide** to meet the President.

大統領に会うために、至る所から人がやってきた。

□□□ **164**

in consequence of

~の結果として

前 as a result of something

何かの結果として

例 **In consequence of** her age, her application was automatically rejected.

年齢を理由に、彼女の応募は自動的にはじかれた。

□□□ **165**

go to extremes

極端に走る

動 to act or be forced to act in a way that is not normal or reasonable

普通でない、または理に適っていない仕方で行動する、あるいは行動するよう強いられる

例 The doctor argues that fasting can be healthy as long as you don't **go to extremes**.

その医師は、絶食は極端に走らない限り健康によいこともあると主張している。

□□□ 166

of late

近ごろ、最近

副 during a recent period of time

最近の期間に

≒ lately, recently

例 You seem to be a bit tired **of late**.

最近、少し疲れているようですね。

□□□ 167

of your (own) choice

自分自身で選んだ

形 that you choose yourself when you have no limits

制限がない中、自分自身で選択する

例 She wants her children to be able to go to the school **of their own choice**.

彼女は、子どもたちに自分で選んだ学校に行ってほしいと思っている。

□□□ 168

to *someone's* liking

〈人〉の好みに合って

形 suitable and enjoyable to someone

誰かに適していてうれしい

例 We hope that this room is **to your liking**.

この部屋があなたの好みに合うとよいのですが。

□□□ 169

do credit to

〈人〉の名誉である

動 to make sure someone is praised or respected

誰かが称賛、あるいは尊敬されるようにする

169句

ⓘ 〈do 人 credit〉の形でも使われる。

例 The fact that they immediately stopped selling the product when they realized it could be dangerous **does credit to** them.

危険かもしれないとわかった時点で、すぐに製品の販売を中止したことは、彼らの評価を高めている。

□□□ **170**

# of your own accord

自分の意志で、
自発的に

圖 without being asked or forced

頼まれたり強制されたりす
ることなく

例 His son decided to wash the dishes **of his own accord**.

彼の息子は自発的に皿洗いを
することにした。

□□□ **171**

this and that

あれこれ、
いろいろなこと

图 various different things

さまざまなこと[もの]

例 Let's get a little bit of **this and that** for the wedding.

結婚式のために、少しあれこれ
買おう。

□□□ **172**

for one

一例として

圖 ① as an example

例として

例 There are many people willing to help you. Ms. Smith, **for one**.

喜んであなたを手伝ってくれる
人はたくさんいるんですよ。ス
ミスさんとか。

個人としては

圖 ② used to emphasize that you are thinking or behaving in a particular way, even if other people are not

ほかの人がそうでなくても、
自分が特定の仕方で考えた
り行動したりしていることを
強調するのに使われる

ⓘ ふつうI, for one の形で使われる。

例 I, **for one**, would prefer to take a flight that leaves in the morning.

私としては、午前発のフライト
に乗るほうがいい。

□□□ 173

on the move

忙しい

形 ① busy and very active

忙しく、非常に活動的な

≒ on the go

例 Sydney is constantly **on the move** because of all of her afterschool activities.

シドニーは、課外活動があれこれあっていつも忙しい。

移動して

② moving from one place to another

ある場所から別の場所へ移動して

≒ on the go

例 There are reports that the rebel army is **on the move**.

反乱軍が移動しているという報告がある。

〈物事が〉進展して

③ making progress

進展して

例 After a slow start, the company he started is finally **on the move**.

彼が立ち上げた会社は、スロースタートの後、やっと動き出した。

□□□ 174

know better than to *do*

～するほど愚かではない

動 to have enough experience and knowledge not to do something

何かをしないだけの十分な経験と知識を持っている

174句

例 You **know better than to** hit your sister just because she took your toy.

お前は、おもちゃを取られたくらいで妹をたたくほど愚かじゃないね。

give rise to

～を引き起こす

動 to be the reason something bad happens

何か悪いことが起こる理由となる

例 Her absence from the party **gave rise to** a huge argument the next day.

彼女がパーティーに来なかったことで、翌日大げんかになった。

be given over to

もっぱら～に使われる

動 to be used for a particular purpose, especially a different one than originally planned

ある特定の目的、特に当初の計画とは異なる目的に使われる

例 This garage **is given over to** creating music.

このガレージはもっぱら音楽制作に使われている。

in earnest

真面目に、本気で

副 ① very seriously and without fooling around

非常に真面目で、ふざけることなく

例 He practices the trombone every day **in earnest**.

彼は毎日真面目にトロンボーンを練習している。

本格的に

② properly and seriously

きちんと、真剣に

例 Your real task begins **in earnest** on Wednesday.

あなたの実質的な仕事は、水曜日に本格的に始まります。

□□□ 178

read between the lines

行間を読む、
言外の意味を読み取る

動 to look for or find a hidden meaning that is not directly stated or obvious

直接述べられていない、または明らかではない隠された意味を、探したり見つけたりする

例 Part of communicating with others is being able to **read between the lines**.

他者とのコミュニケーションの一部は、言外の意味を読み取れることだ。

□□□ 179

go too far

度が過ぎる、やり過ぎる

動 to do something so extreme that it is not acceptable

許容できないほど極端なことをする

≒ go this [that] far

例 You **went too far** when you said that about her mother.

彼女のお母さんについてあなたが言ったことは、言い過ぎでしたよ。

□□□ 180

all but

〜以外全部（のもの［人］）

前 everything or everyone except for something or someone

何かまたは誰かを除くすべてのものまたはすべての人

例 **All but** one of the rooms were damaged in the flood.

一部屋を除いて全室が洪水で損害を受けた。

180句

ほとんど

副 almost completely

ほとんど完全に

例 The event was **all but** over by the time we arrived.

私たちが到着する頃には、イベントはほとんど終わっていた。

□□□ 181

at short notice

直前に

🔊 **without a lot of time or a warning in advance**

事前に多くの時間や警告なしに

ⓘ「直前の」という形容詞の意味もある。

📝 It's impossible for me to design this for you **at short notice**.

直前に言われても、これをデザインしてあげるのは無理です。

□□□ 182

out of control

制御しきれなくなって

🔊 **impossible to be handled or controlled**

処理または制御が不可能で

📝 The party was completely **out of control** when we arrived.

私たちが到着したとき、パーティーは完全に収拾のつかない状態になっていた。

□□□ 183

be concerned with

～とかかわりがある

🔊 ① **to be related to or about something**

何かに関連している、または何かについてである

📝 All of her books **are concerned with** feminist ideas.

彼女の著書はすべてフェミニズムの思想に関連している。

～に関心がある

② **to have an interest in something because you think it is important**

何かを重要だと思い、それに興味を持っている

📝 She has always **been concerned with** how people perceive her.

彼女はいつも、自分が人にどう見られているか気にしている。

□□□ **184**

It is no use *doing*

~しても無駄だ

構 used to tell someone not to do something because it is a waste of time

時間の無駄なので何かをしないようにと誰かに言うのに使われる

例 **It is no use** doing something just because someone tells you to do it.

誰かにやれと言われたからやる、というのでは意味がない。

□□□ **185**

in store for

〈人〉を待ち受けて

形 waiting to happen to someone

誰かに起こるのを待ち構えて

例 There is no telling what the future holds **in store for** us.

将来、何が私たちを待ち受けているかはわからない。

□□□ **186**

lose your temper

かっとなる

動 to become unable to control your anger

怒りを抑えられなくなる

例 Tara easily **loses her temper** when people do things that annoy her.

タラは、人から嫌なことをされるとすぐにかっとなる。

□□□ **187**

take the trouble to *do*

わざわざ~する

187句

動 to do something even though it takes effort and is not easy

努力が必要で、容易なことではないが、それでも何かをする

例 Thank you for **taking the trouble to** make this cake for me.

私のためにわざわざケーキを作ってくれてありがとう。

章末ボキャブラリーチェック

次の語義が表す英熟語を答えてください。

語義	解答	連番
❶ used to show a specific thing that is being talked about	in terms of	155
❷ very seriously and without fooling around	in earnest	177
❸ to look straight at someone who is also looking at you	look in the eye	131
❹ to become successful and rich after being poor	make good	142
❺ used to tell someone not to do something because it is a waste of time	It is no use doing	184
❻ to understand something that is complicated	make sense of	161
❼ to act or be forced to act in a way that is not normal or reasonable	go to extremes	165
❽ used to emphasize that you are thinking or behaving in a particular way, even if other people are not	for one	172
❾ to do something where there is a chance something could go wrong	take a chance	134
❿ various different things	this and that	171
⓫ without a lot of time or a warning in advance	at short notice	181
⓬ used to show how something you are talking about is compared to another thing	in relation to	138
⓭ having already started	under way	129
⓮ to become unable to control your anger	lose your temper	186
⓯ to be related to or about something	be concerned with	183
⓰ usually, or in most situations	as often as not	157
⓱ not at all	not in the least	141
⓲ in a shorter form	for short	147
⓳ showing or saying the opposite	to the contrary	151

語義	解答	連番
❷⓪ stopping someone or something from moving or doing something	<u>in the way</u>	135
❷① in order to help someone	<u>on behalf of</u>	130
❷② to have to deal with something or someone difficult or threatening	<u>be confronted with</u>	144
❷③ busy and very active	<u>on the move</u>	173
❷④ used when making a general statement	<u>by and large</u>	145
❷⑤ because of someone or for someone	<u>on behalf of</u>	130
❷⑥ to be very successful in the future	<u>go far</u>	152
❷⑦ to make sure someone is praised or respected	<u>do credit to</u>	169
❷⑧ to have an interest in something because you think it is important	<u>be concerned with</u>	183
❷⑨ during a recent period of time	<u>of late</u>	166
❸⓪ making progress	<u>on the move</u>	173
❸① to look for or find a hidden meaning that is not directly stated or obvious	<u>read between the lines</u>	178
❸② used to emphasize that something will definitely happen or be true despite something else	<u>in any event</u>	140
❸③ to make someone understand something by saying it aggressively	<u>drive home</u>	162
❸④ to pay attention to someone or something and know what they are doing or where they are	<u>keep track of</u>	153
❸⑤ used to say that you do not believe that something will happen soon or maybe ever	<u>hold your breath</u>	159
❸⑥ related to something	<u>in relation to</u>	138
❸⑦ in complete control of something	<u>on top of</u>	150
❸⑧ to do something so extreme that it is not acceptable	<u>go too far</u>	179
❸⑨ to be less than what was expected or is needed	<u>fall short of</u>	136
❹⓪ as soon as possible	<u>at your earliest convenience</u>	156
❹① to be used for a particular purpose, especially a different one than originally planned	<u>be given over to</u>	176

語義	解答	連番
㊷ suitable and enjoyable to someone	to *someone's* liking	168
㊸ used to add to what you have just said	for that matter	148
㊹ used to say that something was not useful or did not produce a good result	so much for	143
㊺ as an example	for one	172
㊻ in an upright position	on end	128
㊼ without being asked or forced	of your own accord	170
㊽ that you choose yourself when you have no limits	of your (own) choice	167
㊾ not having what you want or need	hard up for	158
㊿ starting and stopping over and over again	on and off	139
(51) as a result of something	in consequence of	164
(52) being in a good situation	well off	132
(53) properly and seriously	in earnest	177
(54) almost completely	all but	180
(55) impossible to be handled or controlled	out of control	182
(56) with some time between	at intervals	137
(57) to do something on purpose, even when it involves extra effort	make a point of *doing*	146
(58) to have enough experience and knowledge not to do something	know better than to *do*	174
(59) instead of someone	on behalf of	130
(60) over a large area	far and wide	163
(61) with the parts that are normally inside on the outside	inside out	154
(62) to do something you have said you would do	make good	142
(63) on the surface of something	on top of	150
(64) everything or everyone except for something or someone	all but	180

語義	解答	連番
❻❺ to earn money from doing something	<u>m</u>a<u>k</u>e <u>m</u>o<u>n</u>e<u>y</u>	160
❻❻ to stop breathing for a short time on purpose	<u>h</u>o<u>l</u>d <u>y</u>o<u>u</u>r <u>b</u>r<u>e</u>a<u>t</u>h	159
❻❼ in addition to something	<u>o</u>n <u>t</u>o<u>p</u> <u>o</u>f	150
❻❽ moving from one place to another	<u>o</u>n <u>t</u>h<u>e</u> <u>m</u>o<u>v</u>e	173
❻❾ very close to someone or something	<u>o</u>n <u>t</u>o<u>p</u> <u>o</u>f	150
❼⓪ having started to move or go somewhere	<u>u</u>n<u>d</u>e<u>r</u> <u>w</u>a<u>y</u>	129
❼❶ with some space between	<u>a</u>t <u>i</u>n<u>t</u>e<u>r</u>v<u>a</u>l<u>s</u>	137
❼❷ to fix, replace, or pay for something you have done wrong or damaged	<u>m</u>a<u>k</u>e <u>g</u>o<u>o</u>d	142
❼❸ for the length of time specified and without stopping	<u>o</u>n <u>e</u>n<u>d</u>	128
❼❹ to do something even though it takes effort and is not easy	<u>t</u>a<u>k</u>e <u>t</u>h<u>e</u> <u>t</u>r<u>o</u>u<u>b</u>l<u>e</u> <u>t</u>o *do*	187
❼❺ having a lot of money	<u>w</u>e<u>l</u>l <u>o</u>f<u>f</u>	132
❼❻ to be the reason something bad happens	<u>g</u>i<u>v</u>e <u>r</u>i<u>s</u>e <u>t</u>o	175
❼❼ used to show you are done talking about something	<u>s</u>o <u>m</u>u<u>c</u>h <u>f</u>o<u>r</u>	143
❼❽ waiting to happen to someone	<u>i</u>n <u>s</u>t<u>o</u>r<u>e</u> <u>f</u>o<u>r</u>	185
❼❾ not able to protect yourself from someone or something because they have control	<u>a</u>t <u>t</u>h<u>e</u> <u>m</u>e<u>r</u>c<u>y</u> <u>o</u>f	149
❽⓪ until and including the present	<u>a</u>s <u>y</u>e<u>t</u>	133

HANG ON (→360)

hangは「ぶら下がる」という意味の
動詞、onは接触、継続を意味す
る副詞／前置詞です。何かにぶら
下がるには、当然接触していなけれ
ばなりませんが、onがつくことで、
ぎゅっとつかまっているニュアンス

が出ます。また、ぶら下がる先が揺れたり折れたりすれば、ぶら下がっている
ものも揺れたり落ちたりしてしまうので、「～次第である、～にかかっている」
という抽象的な意味も出てきます。「ぶら下がり続ける」という継続のイメージ
からは「(苦境を)持ちこたえる」という意味も出てきます。

① (ものに)しっかりつかまる、しがみつく

Hang on to your hats. It's windy!

(帽子を押さえて。風が強いよ!)

② (苦境を)持ちこたえる

I know the procedure is painful, but if you can just **hang on** for couple
more minutes, it will all be over.

(治療は痛いと思うけど、あと2、3分頑張ればすべて終わるからね。)

③ ～次第である、～にかかっている

The future of the company **hangs on** the outcome of this sales
presentation.

(会社の将来は、この営業プレゼンテーションの結果にかかっている。)

Stage 4

Slow and steady wins the race.
急がば回れ。

□□□ **188**

with a view to *doing*

〜する目的で

副 **because you want to do something in the future**

将来何かをしたいので

例 We moved to this city **with a view to** starting a business.

私たちは事業を始める目的で、この市に引っ越してきた。

□□□ **189**

make it

たどり着く；（乗り物などに）間に合う

動 ① **to succeed in getting to a place in time when it was not easy to do so**

容易でなかったけれども、ある場所に時間内に着くのに成功する

例 We won't be able to **make it** unless we take a taxi.

タクシーに乗らないと間に合わないよ。

成功する

② **to be successful at something**

何かで成功する

例 To **make it** in the film industry, you have to be willing to put yourself out there.

映画界で成功するには、積極的に世間に出ていかなければならない。

何とか出席する、都合をつける

③ **to be able to go to an event**

あるイベントに行くことができる

例 Sorry, but we won't be able to **make it** to the party because our daughter is sick.

すみませんが、娘の具合が悪く、パーティーに出席することができません。

□□□ **190**

in principle

（実際はともかく）理論的には

副 ① used to say something is probably possible, but has not been tried yet

まだ試してはいないが、何かがおそらく可能だと述べるのに使われる

≒ theoretically

例 **In principle**, there is no reason why we cannot use different techniques to achieve the same effect.

理論的には、私たちが同じ効果を得るために異なる技術を使うことができないという理由はない。

全体としては

② in general and without a lot of details

一般的に、多くの細かい点は含めずに

例 They have agreed to the terms of the contract **in principle** but still need to sign it.

彼らは契約の条件に全体としては合意したが、まだ署名する必要がある。

□□□ **191**

get on *someone's* nerves

〈人〉の神経に障る

動 to annoy someone, especially by doing a particular thing often

特に特定のことを頻繁に行うことによって、誰かを困らせる

例 The sound of the construction was really **getting on my nerves**.

工事の音は、本当に神経に障った。

□□□ **192**

within reach of

〜の近くに

前 close to something

何かに近い

例 All of the most famous tourist attractions are **within reach of** the hotel.

有名な観光地はすべてホテルの近くにある。

□□□ **193**

fight it out

最後まで戦う[議論する]

動 to argue or fight until you agree

同意するまで議論する、または戦う

例 Instead of talking it over calmly, the two decided to **fight it out**.

2人は冷静に話し合うのではなく、徹底的に議論することにした。

□□□ **194**

be apt to *do*

〜する傾向がある

動 to have a natural tendency to do something

何かをする生来の傾向がある

例 Some of the students **are apt to** hand in their papers late.

レポートの提出が遅れがちな学生もいる。

□□□ **195**

on second thought

よく考えてみると

副 used to say that you have changed your opinion about something

何かについての意見が変わったと言うのに使われる

例 **On second thought**, why don't we go out for ice cream instead?

よく考えてみたら、代わりにアイスクリームを食べに行くのはどう?

□□□ **196**

make do with

〜で間に合わせる

動 to manage to do something with what you have even though it is not ideal

理想的なものではなくても、自分が持っているもので何とかする

ⓘ make do without は「〜なしで済ませる」という意味。

例 We'll just have to **make do with** the clay that we have available.

私たちは今ある粘土で間に合わせるしかないでしょう。

□□□ 197

no better than

~も同然

形 as bad as a specific thing or person

特定のものや人と同じくらいひどい

例 If you abandon your family, then you're **no better than** your father.

家族を見捨てるなら、あなたのお父さんと変わらないよ。

□□□ 198

by name

名前で、名指しで

副 using the name of someone or something

誰かまたは何かの名前を使って

例 Nobody knew the man **by name**.

その男性の名前は誰も知らなかった。

□□□ 199

irrespective of

~に関係なく

前 without thinking about something

何かについて考えずに

≒ regardless of

例 All of our seminars are open to everyone, **irrespective of** university affiliation.

本学のセミナーはすべて、大学の所属に関係なくどなたでもご参加いただけます。

□□□ 200

in the main

概して

副 used to say something is true in most cases

何かがたいていの場合は真実であると述べるのに使われる

200句

≒ in general, mostly

例 Cell phone reception is, **in the main**, reliable here.

ここは概して、携帯電話の電波の受信状況が安定している。

201

think twice

（もう一度）よく考える、熟慮する

動 to think carefully about something before deciding to do it

何かをしようと決める前に、そのことについて慎重に考える

例 You should **think twice** before trying to sneak out.

こっそり抜け出そうとする前に、よく考えたほうがいい。

202

ups and downs

（人生などの）浮き沈み、変化

名 the mixture of good and bad things in a situation

ある状況における、よいことと悪いことの混じり合った状態

例 Despite the **ups and downs**, they've been happily married for over 50 years.

山あり谷ありだったが、2人は50年以上、幸せな結婚生活を送ってきた。

203

work your way

苦労して進む

動 to move slowly and without ease

ゆっくりと苦労して移動する

ⓘ work your way throughも参照。

例 The couple **worked their way** across the bridge carefully.

そのカップルは、注意しながら橋を苦労して渡った。

204

to no purpose

無駄に

副 with no useful results

有用な結果を伴わずに

例 The negotiations for the merger went on for months, but **to no purpose**.

合併に向けた交渉は何か月も続いたが、何の成果もなかった。

□□□ 205

as such

正確な[通常の]意味での

形 in the usual sense

ふつうの意味での

ⓘ 否定文で使われる。

例 It wasn't a job offer **as such**, but they did tell me they'd contact me as soon as a position opens up.

いわゆる内定ではなかったが、彼らは募集があり次第連絡をくれると言った。

□□□ 206

on the spot

即座に

副 ① right away and where something has been mentioned

即座に、何かが言及された場所で

≒ immediately

例 The woman was arrested **on the spot** for assaulting a police officer.

その女性は、警察官への暴行容疑で現行犯逮捕された。

（何かが起こっている）現場で

② in the exact place where something is happening

何かが起こっているまさにその場で

例 Luckily, medical staff **on the spot** were able to stop the bleeding until paramedics arrived.

幸いにも、救急隊員が到着するまで、その場にいた医療スタッフが止血することができた。

206句

（移動せず）その場で

③ without moving from the place where you are

いる場所から動かずに

ⓘ イギリス英語。

例 Running **on the spot** is an easy way to get exercise in a hotel room.

その場で走るのはホテルの部屋で運動する手軽な方法だ。

□□□ **207**

be to blame for

～の責任［罪］がある

🔁 **to be responsible for something bad**

何か悪いことの責任がある

例 Nobody here **is to blame for** what happened that night.

あの夜の出来事の責任は、ここにいる誰にもない。

□□□ **208**

keep an eye on

～から目を離さない

🔁 **to watch or take care of someone or something**

誰かまたは何かを見守る、あるいは世話をする

例 Her parents asked her to **keep an eye on** her little sister while they went to the store.

彼女の両親は、店に行く間、妹から目を離さないように彼女に頼んだ。

□□□ **209**

once and for all

これを最後に、きっぱりと

🔁 **completely and for the last time**

完全に、そして最後に

例 The matter will be decided **once and for all** at tomorrow's trial.

この問題は明日の公判できっぱりと決着がつくだろう。

□□□ **210**

in between

～の合間に

🔁 **in a period of time or space separating two or more points**

2つまたはそれ以上の点を分けている時間または空間の間に

ⓘ 「合間に」という副詞の使い方もある。

例 I have a job interview **in between** my two classes tomorrow.

明日は2つの授業の合間に仕事の面接がある。

□□□ 211

on the job

仕事中で

形 doing a specific job

特定の仕事をしている間

例 Don't bother your father when he's **on the job**.

お父さんが仕事をしているときは、邪魔をしてはいけません。

□□□ 212

have an eye for

～を見る目がある

動 to have a natural ability for seeing and noticing something

何かを見て気づく生来の能力を持っている

例 You really do **have an eye for** stage talent.

あなたは本当に俳優の才能を見る目がありますね。

□□□ 213

come close to *doing*

もう少しで～しそうになる

動 to almost do something

何かをほとんどしそうになる

例 Sandy **came close to** throwing her phone against the wall before she finally calmed down.

サンディは携帯を壁に投げつけそうになったが、最終的に落ち着いた。

□□□ 214

on the verge of

～寸前の、
～の瀬戸際で

214句

前 at the point when something is going to happen soon or is likely to happen soon

何かがすぐに起こる、またはすぐに起こる可能性のある時点で

例 Her father walked in on her when she was **on the verge of** tears.

彼女が泣き出しそうなところに、間が悪く父親が入ってきた。

□□□ 215

by degrees

次第に、徐々に

副 very slowly and gradually

とてもゆっくりと、徐々に

例 **By degrees**, she got herself into an upright position.

彼女は、少しずつ体を真っすぐに起こした。

□□□ 216

hold your tongue

黙っている

動 to stop yourself from saying something even though you want to

何かを言いたいが、言わずにこらえる

例 It's better to **hold your tongue** in some situations.

黙っていたほうがいい場合もある。

□□□ 217

in succession

連続して、続けざまに

副 happening one after the other

次から次へと起こる

≒ in a row

例 That famous gymnast won five championships **in succession**.

その有名な体操選手は、5回連続で選手権で優勝した。

□□□ 218

make a fool of

～を笑いものにする

動 to make someone seem stupid on purpose

意図的に誰かが愚かに見えるようにする

ⓘ make a fool of yourselfも参照。

例 He's never forgiven her for **making a fool of** him in public.

彼は人前で自分をばかにした彼女のことを決して許していない。

□□□ 219

catch *someone's* eye

〈人〉の目を引く

動 to attract someone's attention

誰かの注意を引く

例 While browsing through the store, this red dress **caught my eye**.

店内を見て回っていると、この赤いワンピースが目に止まった。

□□□ 220

in full

全部、省略せずに

副 including every part of something

何かのあらゆる部分を含めて

≒ entirely, completely

例 We must receive payment **in full** before we can send you your order.

ご注文品をお送りする前に、全額お支払いいただかなければなりません。

□□□ 221

as regards

〜に関しては、
〜について言えば

前 relating to something

何かに関して

ⓘ この regard は動詞。

例 **As regards** the question you asked earlier, please speak with Ms. Webster.

先ほどのご質問については、ウェブスターさんとお話しください。

222句

□□□ 222

in spite of yourself

思わず、われ知らず

副 used when you do something even though you did not intend to do it

するつもりはなかったのに何かをするというときに使われる

例 Heather started to cry **in spite of herself**.

ヘザーは思わず泣き出した。

□□□ 223

second to none

何［誰］にも引けを取らない

形 better than all others of the same kind

同種のほかのすべてのものより優れている

≒ the best

例 Grandma's cookies are truly **second to none**.

おばあちゃんのクッキーは、本当に誰にも負けないよ。

□□□ 224

be bent on

〜を決意した

動 to be determined to do something

何かをしようと決意している

例 The kids **are** really **bent on** going to the water park tomorrow.

子どもたちは、明日ウォーターパークに行くことしか頭にない。

□□□ 225

in favor of

〜を支持して、
〜に賛成して

前 ① supporting someone or something

誰かまたは何かを支持して

例 Everyone **in favor of** the motion, please raise your hand now.

動議にに賛成の皆さんは、今手を挙げてください。

〜に有利に（なるように）

② in a way that helps someone

誰かの助けになる仕方で

ⓘ in *someone's* favorの形でも使う。

例 Thankfully the judge ruled **in favor of** our company.

ありがたいことに、裁判官はわが社に有利な判決を下した。

□□□ 226

think better of

〈計画・行為など〉を考
え直してやめる

動 to decide it is better not to do something after thinking about it some more

もう少し考えて、何かをしな
いほうがよいと判断する

例 She **thought better of** disagreeing with her professor in front of the whole class.

彼女は考え直して、クラス全体
の前で教授に反対するのをや
めた。

□□□ 227

for a rainy day

万一に備えて

副 for a time when you really need it

本当にそれを必要とすると
きのために

例 You should save that money **for a rainy day**.

そのお金は万一に備えて取っ
ておくべきだ。

□□□ 228

in progress

進行中で

形 happening now, but not yet finished

今起きているが、まだ終わっ
ていない

例 The test is now **in progress**.

今はテスト中だ。

□□□ 229

at the risk of

〜の危険を冒して

229句

前 used to say you think what you are going to do or say might produce a bad result

自分がしようとしていること
や言おうとしていることがよ
くない結果をもたらすかも
しれないと思っていると述
べるのに使われる

例 **At the risk of** sounding like a complete fool, I think that you should do it.

ばかみたいに聞こえるかもしれ
ませんが、あなたはそうすべき
だと思います。

230

by turns

代わる代わる、次々に

副 changing from one thing to another

あるものから別のものへ変わる

例 He was **by turns** confused, angry, and finally disappointed.

彼はまず混乱し、次に憤慨し、そして最後に失望した。

231

leave something to be desired

物足りない、不満が残る

動 to not be good or high quality

よくない、または質が高くない

ⓘ something の代わりに much や a lot が入ることもある。leave nothing to be desired は「申し分がない」という意味。

例 The taste of this soup **leaves something to be desired**.

このスープの味は何か物足りない。

232

every inch

あらゆる点で、完全に

副 completely and in every way

完全に、そしてあらゆる仕方で

例 With his fancy suit and his expensive watch, he looked **every inch** the CEO.

高級なスーツに高価な時計を身に着けて、彼はいかにもCEOらしく見えた。

隅から隅まで、全体

名 the whole of something

何かの全体

例 **Every inch** of his room is crammed full of books.

彼の部屋は隅々まで本で埋まっている。

□□□ 233

if not

もしそうでないならば

接 ① used to say what will happen if something else does not happen

ほかの何かが起こらなければ何が起こるかを述べるのに使われる

例 Hopefully we'll see you at the family reunion next week, but **if not**, we'll see you at New Years.

来週の家族の集まりで会えるといいんだけど、だめならお正月に会いましょうね。

たとえ〜でないにしても

② used to suggest something may be even more than was first said

何かが、初めに言われたこと以上かもしれないということを示すのに使われる

例 These changes will affect hundreds, **if not** thousands of residents.

これらの変更は、何千人とまでは言わないにせよ、何百人もの住民に影響する。

□□□ 234

at first hand

直接、じかに

副 in a direct way

直接的な仕方で

≒ firsthand

例 If you haven't seen the devastation **at first hand**, then you can't possibly imagine it.

この惨状は、じかに見ていなければ想像すらできないだろう。

235句

□□□ 235

ill at ease

不安で、そわそわして

形 feeling uncomfortable, nervous, and embarrassed

落ち着かなさ、緊張感、ばつの悪さを感じて

⇔ well at ease

例 Ellie had felt **ill at ease** ever since she walked in.

エリーは、入ってきてからずっと居心地の悪さを感じていた。

□□□ 236

take leave of

～にいとまごいをする

動 to say goodbye to someone

誰かに別れを告げる

ⓘ take your leave（いとまごいをする）という使い方もある。

例 It was already dark when they finally **took leave of** their friends and went home.

彼らが友人たちに別れを告げて帰途についたときには、すでに暗くなっていた。

□□□ 237

to the effect that

…という趣旨の

接 used when you are being general rather than being precise

正確であるよりも概略的であるときに使われる

ⓘ to that effect（その趣旨の）という表現も覚えておこう。

例 Her resignation letter said something **to the effect that** she did not feel valued at the company.

彼女の辞表には、会社で評価されている感じがしないという趣旨のことが書かれていた。

□□□ 238

in question

問題［話題］になっている

形 ① used to indicate what exactly is being discussed

正確には何が議論されているのかを示すのに使われる

例 The turkey **in question** has already been put in the oven.

問題の七面鳥は、すでにオーブンに入れられている。

疑わしい、不確かな

② being uncertain or in a state of doubt

不確かで、あるいは不信を抱いていて

例 The future of the school remains **in question**.

その学校の行く末は不確かなままだ。

□□□ 239

kind of

ある程度、いくらか

副 to a small degree

わずかに

≒ slightly, somewhat, sort of

例 The meat was **kind of** burnt, but still tasty.

肉はいくらか焦げていたが、それでもおいしかった。

□□□ 240

hold good

有効である、当てはまる

動 to still exist or be true

まだ存在する、あるいは真実である

例 The promises your previous manager made to you might not **hold good** with this new one.

前の部長がした君との約束は今度の新しい部長では通用しないかもしれない。

□□□ 241

nothing short of

まさに〜、〜そのもの

副 used to emphasize how extreme a situation is

状況がいかに極端であるかを強調するのに使われる

例 It is **nothing short of** ridiculous how long the wait times at this clinic are.

このクリニックの待ち時間の長さは、ばかばかしいとしか言いようがない。

242句

□□□ 242

put to use

〜を使う、利用する

動 to use something in a way that is effective

効果的な仕方で何かを使う

ⓘ 〈put 事物 to use〉の形で使われる。

例 Carli wants to find a job where her language skills can be **put to use**.

カーリは、語学力を生かせる仕事を見つけたいと思っている。

243

as opposed to

~と正反対[対照的]に

前 used to compare things and show they are different from each other

物事を比較し、それらが互いに異なっていることを示すのに使われる

例 In this course, we actually debate philosophy, **as opposed to** just studying it.

この講座では、哲学をただ勉強するのではなく、実際に哲学についてディベートを行います。

244

at heart

根は、本当のところは

副 at the basic level

基本的なところでは

例 He's just a young boy **at heart**.

彼はまだ、根は小さな男の子にすぎない。

245

make allowances for

~を考慮に入れる

動 ① to consider something when you are making a decision or planning something

何かを決定したり計画したりするときに、何かを考慮する

例 If we don't **make allowances for** possible price increases, we may not have enough money.

値上げの可能性を考慮しないと、私たちは資金が足りなくなるかもしれない。

〈人〉（の行為）を大目に見る

② to let someone act in a way that you usually do not approve of because of special reasons

特別な理由により、通常は認めない仕方で誰かを行動させてやる

例 Please note that we will not **make allowances for** people who forget to bring their ticket to the venue.

会場へのチケットの持参をお忘れになった場合、入場はお断りしておりますので、ご了承ください。

□□□ 246

watch your step

足元に気をつける

動 ① to watch where you are walking and move carefully

歩いているところに気を配り、慎重に移動する

≒ mind your step

例 **Watch your step** when going up the stairs.

階段を上るときは、足元にお気をつけください。

用心して行動する

② to be careful of what you say or how you act

発言内容や行動の仕方に気をつける

≒ mind your step

例 You better **watch your step** when talking to the CEO.

CEOと話すときは、言動に気をつけたほうがいいですよ。

□□□ 247

in pairs

2つ[2人]一組で

副 in groups of two

2人一組で

例 Please get **in pairs** and practice the role-play exercise on page 219.

2人一組になって、219ページのロールプレイの練習をしてください。

248句

□□□ 248

be all ears

（人の話などを）熱心に聞いている

動 to be listening closely to what someone has to say because you are interested

興味があるので、誰かが言おうとしていることを注意深く聞いている

例 I**'m all ears** if you think you have a solution to our problem.

私たちの問題を解決する方法があるとお考えなら、ぜひ聞かせてください。

☐☐☐ **249**

in the meantime

その間に、
そうしているうちに

in a period of time between two times or events

2つの時間または出来事の間の期間に

≒ meanwhile

例 Dinner will be ready in 30 minutes. **In the meantime**, why don't you go have a bath?

夕飯は30分でできるよ。その間に、お風呂に入ったら？

☐☐☐ **250**

arm in arm

腕を組んで

with your arm linked to another person's arm

自分の腕とほかの人の腕が組まれた状態で

例 The girls walked **arm in arm** down the street.

その女の子たちは腕を組んで通りを歩いた。

☐☐☐ **251**

be taken aback

びっくりする

to be shocked or surprised by something

何かにショックを受けたり驚いたりする

例 He **was taken aback** by her abrupt singing.

彼女が不意に歌い出して、彼はびっくりした。

☐☐☐ **252**

in the event of

もしも〜の場合には

if something happens

何かが起きたら

例 **In the event of** a natural disaster, please be calm and listen to staff.

自然災害の場合には、落ち着いてスタッフの話をよく聞いてください。

□□□ 253

pull *someone's* leg

〈人〉をからかう、かつぐ

動 to tell someone a lie as a joke

誰かに冗談でうそをつく

例 Don't worry, I was just **pulling your leg**.

心配しないで。あなたをから
かっただけだから。

□□□ 254

ten to one

十中八九、九分九厘

副 used to say that something is very likely

何かが非常に可能性が高い
と言うのに使われる

例 **Ten to one** she'll call me again tomorrow.

十中八九、彼女は明日も電話
をかけてくるだろう。

□□□ 255

out of place

所定の位置でない

形 ① not in the right or usual place

正しい場所またはいつもの
場所にない

⇔ in place

例 Nothing is ever **out of place** in his kitchen.

彼のキッチンは、いつもすべて
のものが所定の場所に置かれ
ている。

255句

場違いな、不適切な

② not suitable for a specific situation

特定の状況に適していない

例 Bob felt **out of place** at a party meant for professionals.

ボブは、プロ向けのパーティー
で場違いな感じがした。

章末ボキャブラリーチェック

次の語義が表す英熟語を答えてください。

語義	解答	連番
❶ the whole of something	every inch	232
❷ the mixture of good and bad things in a situation	ups and downs	202
❸ better than all others of the same kind	second to none	223
❹ happening now, but not yet finished	in progress	228
❺ in general and without a lot of details	in principle	190
❻ completely and for the last time	once and for all	209
❼ in groups of two	in pairs	247
❽ to decide it is better not to do something after thinking about it some more	think better of	226
❾ to have a natural ability for seeing and noticing something	have an eye for	212
❿ supporting someone or something	in favor of	225
⓫ used to say that you have changed your opinion about something	on second thought	195
⓬ in the usual sense	as such	205
⓭ doing a specific job	on the job	211
⓮ right away and where something has been mentioned	on the spot	206
⓯ relating to something	as regards	221
⓰ used when you are being general rather than being precise	to the effect that	237
⓱ with your arm linked to another person's arm	arm in arm	250
⓲ to attract someone's attention	catch someone's eye	219
⓳ changing from one thing to another	by turns	230
⓴ used to suggest something may be even more than was first said	if not	233
㉑ without thinking about something	irrespective of	199

語義	解答	連番
㉒ to a small degree	k i n d o f	239
㉓ very slowly and gradually	b y d e g r e e s	215
㉔ for a time when you really need it	f o r a r a i n y d a y	227
㉕ in a period of time or space separating two or more points	i n b e t w e e n	210
㉖ to watch or take care of someone or something	k e e p a n e y e o n	208
㉗ as bad as a specific thing or person	n o b e t t e r t h a n	197
㉘ without moving from the place where you are	o n t h e s p o t	206
㉙ to succeed in getting to a place in time when it was not easy to do so	m a k e i t	189
㉚ to use something in a way that is effective	p u t t o u s e	242
㉛ to have a natural tendency to do something	b e a p t t o *d o*	194
㉜ used to emphasize how extreme a situation is	n o t h i n g s h o r t o f	241
㉝ to argue or fight until you agree	f i g h t i t o u t	193
㉞ to be able to go to an event	m a k e i t	189
㉟ used to say something is probably possible, but has not been tried yet	i n p r i n c i p l e	190
㊱ to be successful at something	m a k e i t	189
㊲ in the exact place where something is happening	o n t h e s p o t	206
㊳ to move slowly and without ease	w o r k y o u r w a y	203
㊴ to stop yourself from saying something even though you want to	h o l d y o u r t o n g u e	216
㊵ to not be good or high quality	l e a v e s o m e t h i n g t o b e d e s i r e d	231
㊶ used when you do something even though you did not intend to do it	i n s p i t e o f y o u r s e l f	222
㊷ happening one after the other	i n s u c c e s s i o n	217
㊸ feeling uncomfortable, nervous, and embarrassed	i l l a t e a s e	235
㊹ in a way that helps someone	i n f a v o r o f	225
㊺ close to something	w i t h i n r e a c h o f	192

語義	解答	連番
㉠ to think carefully about something before deciding to do it	think twice	201
㉡ not suitable for a specific situation	out of place	255
㉢ to be careful of what you say or how you act	watch your step	246
㉣ to make someone seem stupid on purpose	make a fool of	218
㉤ using the name of someone or something	by name	198
㉥ to watch where you are walking and move carefully	watch your step	246
㉦ to annoy someone, especially by doing a particular thing often	get on someone's nerves	191
㉧ completely and in every way	every inch	232
㉨ to manage to do something with what you have even though it is not ideal	make do with	196
㉩ to consider something when you are making a decision or planning something	make allowances for	245
㉪ being uncertain or in a state of doubt	in question	238
㉫ to still exist or be true	hold good	240
㉬ in a direct way	at first hand	234
㉭ used to say something is true in most cases	in the main	200
㉠ to let someone act in a way that you usually do not approve of because of special reasons	make allowances for	245
㉡ to tell someone a lie as a joke	pull someone's leg	253
㉢ used to compare things and show they are different from each other	as opposed to	243
㉣ at the basic level	at heart	244
㉤ used to say what will happen if something else does not happen	if not	233
㉥ used to say that something is very likely	ten to one	254
㉦ with no useful results	to no purpose	204
㉧ if something happens	in the event of	252
㉨ because you want to do something in the future	with a view to doing	188

語義	解答	連番
❻❾ at the point when something is going to happen soon or is likely to happen soon	<u>o</u><u>n</u> <u>t</u><u>h</u><u>e</u> <u>v</u><u>e</u><u>r</u><u>g</u><u>e</u> <u>o</u><u>f</u>	214
❼⓿ to almost do something	<u>c</u><u>o</u><u>m</u><u>e</u> <u>c</u><u>l</u><u>o</u><u>s</u><u>e</u> <u>t</u><u>o</u> <u>doing</u>	213
❼❶ not in the right or usual place	<u>o</u><u>u</u><u>t</u> <u>o</u><u>f</u> <u>p</u><u>l</u><u>a</u><u>c</u><u>e</u>	255
❼❷ in a period of time between two times or events	<u>i</u><u>n</u> <u>t</u><u>h</u><u>e</u> <u>m</u><u>e</u><u>a</u><u>n</u><u>t</u><u>i</u><u>m</u><u>e</u>	249
❼❸ to be shocked or surprised by something	<u>b</u><u>e</u> <u>t</u><u>a</u><u>k</u><u>e</u><u>n</u> <u>a</u><u>b</u><u>a</u><u>c</u><u>k</u>	251
❼❹ to be determined to do something	<u>b</u><u>e</u> <u>b</u><u>e</u><u>n</u><u>t</u> <u>o</u><u>n</u>	224
❼❺ used to indicate what exactly is being discussed	<u>i</u><u>n</u> <u>q</u><u>u</u><u>e</u><u>s</u><u>t</u><u>i</u><u>o</u><u>n</u>	238
❼❻ to be listening closely to what someone has to say because you are interested	<u>b</u><u>e</u> <u>a</u><u>l</u><u>l</u> <u>e</u><u>a</u><u>r</u><u>s</u>	248
❼❼ to be responsible for something bad	<u>b</u><u>e</u> <u>t</u><u>o</u> <u>b</u><u>l</u><u>a</u><u>m</u><u>e</u> <u>f</u><u>o</u><u>r</u>	207
❼❽ including every part of something	<u>i</u><u>n</u> <u>f</u><u>u</u><u>l</u><u>l</u>	220
❼❾ used to say you think what you are going to do or say might produce a bad result	<u>a</u><u>t</u> <u>t</u><u>h</u><u>e</u> <u>r</u><u>i</u><u>s</u><u>k</u> <u>o</u><u>f</u>	229
❽⓿ to say goodbye to someone	<u>t</u><u>a</u><u>k</u><u>e</u> <u>l</u><u>e</u><u>a</u><u>v</u><u>e</u> <u>o</u><u>f</u>	236

PICK UP(→403)

pickは「〜を摘む、つまみ取る」という意味の動詞、upは「上へ」を意味する副詞で、組み合わせると「〜を拾い上げる、持ち上げる」という意味になります。駅などで待っている人を「拾い上げる」イメージからは

「〈人〉を(乗り物で)迎えに行く」という意味が、店でものを「拾い上げる」イメージからは「〜を手に入れる、買う」という意味が、さらに抽象的に技術や知識などを「拾い上げる」イメージからは「〈技術・知識など〉を身につける」という意味が出てきます。なお、日本語では「選び出す」の意味で「ピックアップする」という言葉を使いますが、英語ではpick outと言います。

①〜を拾い上げる、持ち上げる

If you saw a $1 bill on the ground, would you **pick** it **up**?

(地面に1ドル札が落ちていたら、あなたは拾いますか。)

②〈人〉を(乗り物で)迎えに行く

Usually my wife **picks** me **up** from the airport.

(いつもは妻が空港に迎えに来てくれる。)

③〜を手に入れる、買う

Could you **pick up** some mozzarella cheese on your way home from work?

(仕事の帰りにモッツァレラチーズを買ってきてくれませんか。)

④〈技術・知識など〉を身につける

I thought I'd **pick up** Chinese naturally by living here, but I still can't speak it at all.

(ここに住んでいれば自然に中国語が身につくと思っていたけど、まだ全然話せない。)

Stage 5

Never put off till tomorrow what you can do today.
今日できることを明日まで延ばすな。

□□□ 256

take pains

骨を折る、苦労する

動 to put in a lot of effort to do something

何かをするために多くの努力を費す

≒ go to great pains

例 He **took** great **pains** to move his entire family from Pakistan to the U.S.

彼は、大変な苦労をして家族全員をパキスタンから米国に移住させた。

□□□ 257

in demand

需要がある

形 wanted by a lot of people

多くの人に求められている

例 This coin is **in** high **demand** among collectors.

このコインはコレクターの間で需要が高い。

□□□ 258

go astray

〈ものが〉行方不明になる、盗まれる

動 ① to become lost

失われる

例 Her gift to her family **went astray** in the post.

彼女からの家族へのプレゼントは、郵送中に行方知れずになってしまった。

道を誤る、失敗する

② to go the wrong way or have the wrong result

間違った方向に進む、または間違った結果になる

例 Even the most meticulously planned events can **go astray**.

極めて綿密に計画されたイベントでも、失敗することはある。

☐☐☐ 259

believe it or not

信じないかもしれないが

圖 used to say something is true but surprising

何かが真実だが驚くべきことだと言うのに使われる

例 **Believe it or not**, your grandfather used to be a race car driver.

信じないかもしれないけど、お前のおじいちゃんはカーレーサーだったんだよ。

☐☐☐ 260

get nowhere

うまくいかない

圖 to make no progress or not have any success

進歩しない、または不成功に終わる

例 She decided to go to sleep because she was **getting nowhere** with her paper.

彼女は、論文がうまく進まないので、あきらめて寝ることにした。

☐☐☐ 261

at large

〈危険な人物・動物などが〉自由で

圏 ① not captured and free

捕らえられておらず、自由な

261句

例 The person who killed them is still **at large**.

彼らを殺した人物は、今なお逃亡中だ。

一般の、全体としての

② as a whole

全体としての

例 Everyone's opinion **at large** is that there should be vegetarian options at the party.

パーティーにはベジタリアンメニューもあったほうがよいというのが、全体としての意見だ。

□□□ 262

on good terms with

〜と仲がよくて

形 having a good relationship with someone

誰かと良好な関係を持って

⇔ on bad terms with

例 Tanya has always been **on good terms with** the rest of her family.

ターニャはいつも、ほかの家族と仲よくしてきた。

□□□ 263

to make a long story short

早い話が、
かいつまんで言うと

副 used to say that you are only going to mention the main information without including all the details

すべての詳細は含めず、主要な情報のみに言及するつもりだと言うために使われる

ⓘ イギリス英語では to cut a long story short と言う。

例 **To make a long story short**, she isn't coming tonight.

早い話、彼女は今夜は来ないんだ。

□□□ 264

be hard on

〈人〉につらく当たる

動 ① to criticize someone unfairly

誰かを不当に批判する

例 Don't you think you're **being** too **hard on** her?

あなたは彼女につらく当たりすぎだと思いませんか。

〜を痛める、だめにする

② to have a bad effect on something

何かに悪影響を与える

例 Losing a job can **be hard on** any relationship.

失業は、何かと人間関係を損なうことがある。

□□□ 265

be possessed of

〈能力・性質〉を備えて
いる

動 to have a specific quality or feature

特定の品質または特徴を持つ

例 He **was possessed of** brilliant composing skills.

彼は、素晴らしい作曲のスキル
を持っていた。

□□□ 266

by halves

中途半端に、不完全に

**動 in an incomplete way or with very little
effort**

不完全な仕方で、またはほ
とんど努力せずに

ⓘ ふつう否定文で使われる。

例 West has never been one to do anything **by halves**.

ウェストは、どんなことも中途半
端にやるような人間ではない。

□□□ 267

take sides

味方する

**動 to show support for someone in an
argument**

議論において誰かへの支持
を示す

268句

例 Don't look at me to **take sides** in this argument.

けんかで自分の味方になって
もらおうとしてこっちを見ない
でよ。

□□□ 268

by leaps and bounds

急速に、飛躍的に

副 very quickly and in large amounts

とても速く、大量に

ⓘ in leaps and boundsとも言う。

例 She has been making progress **by leaps and bounds**.

彼女は飛躍的に進歩してきて
いる。

□□□ 269

catch your breath

息をのむ

動 ① to stop breathing for a moment because you were scared, shocked, or surprised

怖がったり、ショックを受けたり、驚いたりして、一瞬呼吸を止める

例 Audience members **caught their breath** as the acrobat hung from the wire.

観客は曲芸師がワイヤーからぶら下がると息をのんだ。

一息つく、呼吸を整える

② to rest until you can breathe normally again

再びふつうに呼吸できるようになるまで休む

例 Let's slow down for a bit so I can **catch my breath**.

私が呼吸を整えられるように、少しペースを落としましょう。

□□□ 270

word for word

一言一句変えずに

副 ① using the exact same words

まったく同じ言葉を使って

例 He copied his sister's essay **word for word**.

彼は、姉のレポートを一言一句変えずに書き写した。

逐語的に

② using words with the exact same meaning

まったく同じ意味の言葉を使って

≒ word by word

例 A text translated **word for word** will not read smoothly.

逐語的に訳されたテキストは、スムーズに読めない。

□□□ 271

out of hand

手に負えない

形 not controlled well

うまくコントロールされていない

≒ out of control

例 The children at the daycare are **out of hand**.

その保育園の子どもたちは手に負えない。

すぐに、即座に

副 without considering what was suggested

提案されたことを考慮せずに

例 Her theories were dismissed **out of hand** before she could even explain them fully.

彼女の理論は、十分に説明すらできないうちに、あっさり否定されてしまった。

□□□ 272

at stake

賭けられて、
危険にさらされて

形 likely to be lost or harmed if something fails

何かが失敗すると、失われる、または損害を受ける可能性のある

273句

例 Your scholarship is **at stake** if you don't get your grades up soon.

すぐに成績を上げないと、奨学金が危なくなります。

□□□ 273

wide of the mark

的を外れて；
見当違いで

形 inaccurate by a large amount

大幅に不正確な

≒ off the mark

例 The latest polls seem to be pretty **wide of the mark**.

最新の世論調査はかなり的外れなようだ。

☐☐☐ **274**

take to your heels

一目散に逃げる

動 to run away from someone or something

誰かまたは何かから逃げる

例 As soon as the thief saw the police, he **took to his heels**.

泥棒は警察を見るとすぐ、一目散に逃げた。

☐☐☐ **275**

call it a day

（仕事などを）切り上げる、終わりにする

動 to stop working, especially because you have done enough, are tired, etc.

特にもう十分にやった、疲れたなどの理由で、仕事するのをやめる

例 Let's **call it a day** and go get something to eat.

今日はもう終わりにして、何か食べに行こう。

☐☐☐ **276**

none other than

ほかならぬ

副 used to emphasize someone involved in something is famous, impressive, etc.

何かに関わっている人が、有名である、印象的であるといったことを強調するために使われる

例 The man I met at the shopping center turned out to be **none other than** a famous baseball player.

私がショッピングセンターで出会った男性は、何と有名な野球選手だとわかった。

☐☐☐ **277**

under your breath

小声で

副 quietly so that others cannot hear you

ほかの人に聞こえないように静かに

例 Olaf complained **under his breath** about the price of the phone.

オラフは小声で、電話代について不満を言った。

□□□ 278

to death

死ぬまで〜する、
〜して死ぬ

副 ① used to say how someone died or was killed

誰かがどのように死んだか、
または殺されたかを言うの
に使われる

例 Police announced that the person was beaten **to death** by a group of people.

警察は、その人物は集団に殴
られて死亡したと発表した。

死ぬほど、ひどく

② used to emphasize a strong feeling or emotion

強い気持ちや感情を強調す
るために使われる

例 You scared me **to death** with that mask!

その仮面、怖くて死ぬかと思った！

□□□ 279

be endowed with

〜に恵まれている

動 to have a particular quality, especially a good one

特定の資質、特によい資質
を持っている

例 Even at a very young age, it was apparent that she **was endowed with** extremely high intelligence.

彼女はとても小さい頃から、非
常に高い知能を持っていること
が明らかだった。

280句

□□□ 280

in want of

〜が必要で

形 wanting or needing something

何かを欲している、または
必要としている

例 Mimi's car is **in want of** repair.

ミミの車は修理が必要だ。

give way

崩れる、壊れる

動 ① to break or fall down

壊れる、または倒れる

例 The rotten floor **gave way** under her weight.

その腐った床は彼女の重みで抜けた。

② to agree to do what someone else wants instead of what you want

譲歩する、屈する

自分が望むことではなく、ほかの人が望むことをするのに同意する

≒ yield

例 Ignatius refused to **give way** despite his sister's demands.

イグネイシャスは、姉の要求にもかかわらず、譲らなかった。

③ to be replaced by something else

とって代わられる

ほかの何かに置き換えられる

例 Traditional wooden buildings have **given way** to more modern concrete ones.

伝統的な木造建築は、より現代的なコンクリート製の建築にとって代わられてきた。

out of the blue

突然、出し抜けに

副 unexpectedly and without warning

予期せず、前触れもなく

例 Her cousins came to visit her **out of the blue**.

いとこたちが突然、彼女の元を訪ねてきた。

□□□ 283

take effect

〈法律などが〉効力を発する

動 ① to start to apply

適用され始める

≒ come into effect, go into effect

例 New countermeasures will **take effect** beginning tomorrow.

新しい対策が明日から実施される。

〈薬などが〉効く

② to begin to have the intended result

意図した結果が得られ始める

例 The treatment finally seems to be starting to **take effect**.

ようやく治療の効果が出始めたようだ。

□□□ 284

for the life of me

どうしても

副 used to say that you cannot do something no matter how hard you try

どんなに一生懸命やってみても何かができないことを言うのに使われる

285句

ⓘ 通例can'tと共に使われる。

例 I can't remember her name **for the life of me**.

彼女の名前がどうしても思い出せない。

□□□ 285

from A to Z

初めから終わりまで、完全に

副 including everything

すべてを含めて

例 In this course, we'll study the history of music **from A to Z**.

このコースでは音楽史全体を学びます。

286
in short supply

不足して

形 available only in small amounts

少量しか手に入らない

例 That medication is unfortunately **in short supply**.

その薬は残念ながら不足している。

287
put pressure on

〈人〉を圧迫する、
〈人〉に圧力をかける

動 to try to persuade someone to do something

誰かに何かをするよう説得しようとする

例 Fiona **put** a lot of **pressure on** her manager to allow everyone to go home early on Fridays.

金曜日は全員が早く帰れるよう、フィオナは上司に多くの圧力をかけた。

288
a touch of

少量の

形 a small amount of

少しの量の

例 Adding **a touch of** instant coffee to a chocolate cake will make it taste better.

チョコレートケーキに少量のインスタントコーヒーを加えると、よりおいしくなる。

289
sort of

いくぶん、ちょっと

副 to a small degree

わずかに

≒ slightly, somewhat, kind of

例 Gregory is only **sort of** ready to take his exams.

グレゴリーは試験を受ける準備がほんの少ししかできていない。

126

□□□ 290

in place

正しい[適切な]位置に

形 ① in the correct position

正しい位置に

⇔ out of place

例 All the desks are **in place** for the exam.

机はすべて、試験のために正しい位置に並べられている。

準備[環境]が整って

② ready to be used

使われる準備ができて

例 The budget has already been approved and the money is **in place**.

予算はすでに承認され、資金も準備が整っている。

□□□ 291

the other way around

逆に

副 in the opposite direction or order

反対の方向または順番に

例 To open it, you need to twist it **the other way around**.

それを開けるには逆向きにひねる必要があります。

291句

その逆(のケース)

名 the opposite of what you have already said

すでに言ったことと反対のこと

例 I think that what you have said is **the other way around**.

あなたがおっしゃっていたことは、その逆だと思います。

□□□ **292**

fall victim to

〜の犠牲になる、
被害に遭う

動 to be hurt, cheated, or killed by someone or something

誰かまたは何かに傷つけられたり、だまされたり、殺されたりする

例 Don't let yourself **fall victim to** someone like that.

あんな奴の犠牲にならないようにね。

□□□ **293**

call names

〈人〉の悪口を言う

動 to use offensive words to describe someone

誰かを描写するのに侮辱的な言葉を使う

ⓘ 〈call 人 names〉の形で使われる。

例 A lot of his classmates **called him names** when he was a child.

彼が子どもの頃、多くの同級生は彼の悪口を言った。

□□□ **294**

be cut out for

〜に向いている

動 to have the qualities and abilities needed to do something

何かをするのに必要な資質と能力を持っている

例 Zoey **is**n't really **cut out for** teaching little kids.

ゾーイは小さい子どもを教えるのにあまり向いていない。

□□□ **295**

lose heart

元気をなくす、
意気消沈する

動 to stop hoping for something or believing you are able to do something

何かを期待したり、何かができると信じたりするのをやめる

例 She never **lost heart**, even though studying on her own was really difficult.

独学で勉強するのは本当に大変だったが、彼女は決してくじけなかった。

□□□ 296

come in handy

（いざというとき）役に
立つ

動 to be useful

有用である

例 These tools might **come in handy** someday, so you should keep them.

これらの道具はいつか役に立つかもしれないので、持っていたほうがいいですよ。

□□□ 297

true to life

実物そっくりの、
真に迫った

形 seeming real instead of fake or invented

偽物や作り物ではなく、本物のように見える

例 Her novels are all very **true to life**.

彼女の小説はどれも、とても真に迫っている。

□□□ 298

in a row

連続して、立て続けに

副 happening many times one after the other

次から次へと何度も起こる

299句

≒ consecutively, in succession

ⓘ 「1列に」という意味もある。

例 He lost the game three times **in a row**.

彼は3回連続で試合に負けた。

□□□ 299

in line with

〜と一致して

前 in agreement with something

何かに一致して

例 Unfortunately, pay doesn't seem to increase **in line with** increasing living expenses.

残念ながら、生活費の上昇に合わせて賃金が増えるということはなさそうだ。

MP3 300-302

□□□ **300**

go a long way toward

動 to help achieve something

例 Studying would **go a long way toward** your goal of being fluent in Polish.

〜に大いに役立つ

何かを達成するのを助ける

勉強すれば、ポーランド語を流ちょうに話せるようになるというあなたの目標に大いに役立つだろう。

□□□ **301**

work your way through

動 to achieve something over time by working

ⓘ work your way も参照。

例 **Work your way through** the math problems one by one, and the concepts will start to make sense.

苦労して〜を完了させる

取り組むことで時間をかけて何かを達成する

数学の問題を1つずつ解いていくと、概念が理解できるようになります。

□□□ **302**

get it

動 ① to understand someone or something

例 Sorry, but I still don't **get it**.

わかる、理解する

誰かまたは何かを理解する

すみませんが、まだよくわかりません。

叱られる、罰を受ける

② to be punished for something

例 You're going to **get it** if a teacher catches you smoking on campus!

何かのことで罰せられる

校内でタバコを吸っているところを先生に見つかったら、叱られるよ！

□□□ 303

make a face

顔をしかめる

動 ① to produce an expression on your face that shows you dislike someone or something

誰かまたは何かが嫌いであることを示す表情を顔に浮かべる

例 Helga **made a face** when she put the blue cheese in her mouth.

ヘルガはブルーチーズを口に入れたとき、顔をしかめた。

（笑わせようと）変な顔をする

② to produce an expression on your face to make someone laugh

誰かを笑わせるために顔に表情を浮かべる

例 Wendy **made a face** at the baby, and she laughed.

ウェンディが赤ちゃんに変な顔をすると、赤ちゃんは笑った。

□□□ 304

be dying to *do*

〜したくてたまらない

305句

動 to really want to do something

本当に何かをしたい

例 Kyle **is dying to** go to the signing event tomorrow.

カイルは、明日のサイン会に行きたくて仕方がない。

□□□ 305

come to think of it

そう言えば、考えてみると

副 used to indicate something you have just realized or remembered

今気づいた、または思い出したことを示すために使われる

例 **Come to think of it**, weren't you a lawyer when you were younger?

そういえば、若い頃弁護士だったんじゃないの？

□□□ **306**

to no avail

無駄に

副 **with almost no or no success**

ほとんどまたはまったく成功せずに

例 They searched for the missing file **to no avail**.

彼らは行方不明のファイルを探したが、無駄だった。

□□□ **307**

be all the rage

大人気である、ブームになっている

動 **to be very popular and fashionable**

非常に人気があり流行している

例 Loose socks used to **be all the rage** with teenage girls.

ルーズソックスはかつて、10代の女の子たちの間で大人気だった。

□□□ **308**

turn your back on

〜に背を向ける

動 ① **to move your body so that your back is facing someone or something**

自分の背中が誰かまたは何かに向くように体を動かす

例 Sylvia **turned her back on** her friend to hide her angry face.

シルヴィアは怒った顔を隠すため友人に背を向けた。

〜を見放す、見捨てる

② **to refuse to help, support, or be involved with someone or something**

誰かまたは何かを助けたり、支援したりしたり、関わったりすることを拒否する

例 He **turned his back on** his faith when he was in his 40s and never looked back.

彼は40代のときに信仰を捨て、以後振り返ることはなかった。

□□□ **309**

cut a ~ figure

~に見える

動 to have a particular appearance

特定の外観を持つ

ⓘ ~には形容詞が入る。

例 Mason **cut a** nice **figure** in his uniform.

メイソンは制服を着ると素敵に見えた。

□□□ **310**

behind the times

時代遅れで、流行遅れで

形 not knowing about what is current

今の流行について知らない

≒ outdated

例 Their bakery has slowly fallen **behind the times**.

彼らのパン屋は、少しずつ時代遅れになってきた。

□□□ **311**

go out of your way to *do*

わざわざ~する

動 to make a special effort to do something

何かをするために特別な努力をする

312句

例 You shouldn't **go out of your way to** help people who wouldn't do the same for you.

あなたに同じことをしてくれないような人々をわざわざ助けるべきではありません。

□□□ **312**

pay heed to

~に注意を払う

動 to pay attention to something and think about it carefully

何かに注意を払い、それについて慎重に考える

例 You must **pay heed to** the circumstances of others when making a decision.

何かを決めるときは、ほかの人の状況に注意を払わなければなりません。

章末ボキャブラリーチェック

次の語義が表す英熟語を答えてください。

語義	解答	連番
❶ available only in small amounts	in short supply	286
❷ very quickly and in large amounts	by leaps and bounds	268
❸ used to emphasize a strong feeling or emotion	to death	278
❹ to become lost	go astray	258
❺ the opposite of what you have already said	the other way around	291
❻ used to indicate something you have just realized or remembered	come to think of it	305
❼ to a small degree	sort of	289
❽ using the exact same words	word for word	270
❾ ready to be used	in place	290
❿ to rest until you can breathe normally again	catch your breath	269
⓫ to criticize someone unfairly	be hard on	264
⓬ to help achieve something	go a long way toward	300
⓭ to have a particular quality, especially a good one	be endowed with	279
⓮ to produce an expression on your face that shows you dislike someone or something	make a face	303
⓯ to have a specific quality or feature	be possessed of	265
⓰ to run away from someone or something	take to your heels	274
⓱ to make no progress or not have any success	get nowhere	260
⓲ to move your body so that your back is facing someone or something	turn your back on	308
⓳ to stop working, especially because you have done enough, are tired, etc.	call it a day	275
⓴ used to say something is true but surprising	believe it or not	259

語義	解答	連番
㉑ to be hurt, cheated, or killed by someone or something	fall victim to	292
㉒ to stop breathing for a moment because you were scared, shocked, or surprised	catch your breath	269
㉓ to achieve something over time by working	work your way through	301
㉔ including everything	from A to Z	285
㉕ to be punished for something	get it	302
㉖ with almost no or no success	to no avail	306
㉗ using words with the exact same meaning	word for word	270
㉘ used to say that you cannot do something no matter how hard you try	for the life of me	284
㉙ likely to be lost or harmed if something fails	at stake	272
㉚ used to say how someone died or was killed	to death	278
㉛ to agree to do what someone else wants instead of what you want	give way	281
㉜ to pay attention to something and think about it carefully	pay heed to	312
㉝ inaccurate by a large amount	wide of the mark	273
㉞ a small amount of	a touch of	288
㉟ to produce an expression on your face to make someone laugh	make a face	303
㊱ in the correct position	in place	290
㊲ used to say that you are only going to mention the main information without including all the details	to make a long story short	263
㊳ to really want to do something	be dying to *do*	304
㊴ having a good relationship with someone	on good terms with	262
㊵ wanted by a lot of people	in demand	257
㊶ not captured and free	at large	261
㊷ to be replaced by something else	give way	281

❸ to have the qualities and abilities needed to do something — be cut out for — 294

❹ to understand someone or something — get it — 302

❺ seeming real instead of fake or invented — true to life — 297

❻ to go the wrong way or have the wrong result — go astray — 258

❼ happening many times one after the other — in a row — 298

❽ to have a bad effect on something — be hard on — 264

❾ to have a particular appearance — cut a ～ figure — 309

❺⓪ to make a special effort to do something — go out of your way to do — 311

❺① used to emphasize someone involved in something is famous, impressive, etc. — none other than — 276

❺② to try to persuade someone to do something — put pressure on — 287

❺③ in an incomplete way or with very little effort — by halves — 266

❺④ quietly so that others cannot hear you — under your breath — 277

❺⑤ not knowing about what is current — behind the times — 310

❺⑥ unexpectedly and without warning — out of the blue — 282

❺⑦ without considering what was suggested — out of hand — 271

❺⑧ to stop hoping for something or believing you are able to do something — lose heart — 295

❺⑨ in agreement with something — in line with — 299

❻⓪ wanting or needing something — in want of — 280

❻① to use offensive words to describe someone — call names — 293

❻② not controlled well — out of hand — 271

❻③ to break or fall down — give way — 281

❻④ to start to apply — take effect — 283

❻⑤ in the opposite direction or order — the other way around — 291

語義	解答	連番
⑯ to begin to have the intended result	take effect	283
⑰ to show support for someone in an argument	take sides	267
⑱ as a whole	at large	261
⑲ to be very popular and fashionable	be all the rage	307
⑳ to put in a lot of effort to do something	take pains	256
㉑ to refuse to help, support, or be involved with someone or something	turn your back on	308
㉒ to be useful	come in handy	296

SETTLE DOWN (→444)

settleは語源的に「座る；〜を座らせる」という意味の動詞、downは「下へ」という意味の副詞で、組み合わせると「落ち着く；〜を落ち着かせる」という意味を表します。何かざわざわしていたものが静まる

イメージです。「〈気持ちなどが〉落ち着く」という意味や、ベッドやソファなどに寝転がったり座ったりして「身を落ち着ける」という意味、さらには結婚して「身を固める」という意味などを表します。下には挙げていませんが、どこかに定住して「身を落ち着ける」という意味もあります。

①〈気持などが〉落ち着く

Make sure to wait until the audience **settles down** before you start speaking.

（聴衆が落ち着くまで待ってから、話を始めるようにしてください。）

②身を落ち着ける

She just wanted to **settle down** on the couch and watch movies all day.

（彼女はソファに腰を下ろして、一日中映画を見ていたかっただけだ。）

③身を固める

His parents have been asking him to **settle down** for years, but he's still out traveling the world.

（両親は何年も身を落ち着けてほしいと言っているが、彼はまだ世界中を旅している。）

Stage 6

When the going gets tough, the tough get going.
困難なときが力の見せどき。

313
deprive of
《deprive 人・事物 of 事物》

〜から…を奪う

to take something away from someone or something, or prevent them from getting it

誰かまたは何かから何かを奪う、または彼らがそれを手に入れるのを妨げる

例 Many people are unfortunately **deprived of** safe living conditions.

残念ながら、多くの人々が安全な生活環境を奪われている。

314
devote yourself to
《devote yourself to 人・事物》

〜に専念する

to give most of your time and energy to someone or something

誰かまたは何かに自分の時間とエネルギーのほとんどを捧げる

例 **Devote yourself to** your studies and you will see the results.

勉強に専念すれば、結果は出ますよ。

315
get through with
《get through with 事物》

〈困難な仕事など〉を終える

to finish doing something

何かをやり終える

例 If you **get through with** all your chores, we can go out to lunch.

あなたの用事が全部済んだら、ランチに出かけられます。

316
pass on to
《pass 事物 on to 人 / passe on 事物 to 人》

〈情報など〉を〜に伝える

to give something to someone, especially after receiving it from someone else or using it yourself

特にほかの人から何かを受け取った後、または自分で使った後、誰かにそれを与える

例 Her father asked her to **pass on** a message **to** her brother.

彼女の父親は、弟への伝言を彼女に言付けた。

□□□ **317**

come up with
《come up with 事物》

〈考え・解決策など〉を
出す、思いつく

to think of an idea or answer to something

何かに対する考えや答えを
考え出す

例 The marketing director has asked us to **come up with**
some new ideas.

マーケティング部長は、新しい
アイデアを出すよう私たちに求
めた。

□□□ **318**

put up with
《put up with 人・事物》

〜を我慢する、耐える

to accept something or someone that is not pleasant

楽しくない何かや誰かを受
け入れる

≒ tolerate

例 He has to **put up with** his little sister's crying because
she's just a baby.

妹はまだ赤ちゃんなので、彼は
妹が泣くのを我慢しなければ
ならない。

319句

□□□ **319**

attend to
《attend to 事物》

〜に対処する

to deal with something

何かに対処する

例 There are a few things we must **attend to** before the
meeting tomorrow.

明日の会議の前に、処理しなけれ
ばならないことがいくつかある。

《attend to 人》

〈人〉の世話をする

to help or speak to someone, especially a customer or guest

誰か、特に顧客やゲストを
手助けしたり、彼らに言葉
をかけたりする

≒ serve

例 Her manager asked her to **attend to** the customer
waiting by the cash register.

彼女の上司は、レジのそばで
待っている客に対応するよう彼
女に頼んだ。

320

resort to
《resort to 事物》

to do something because you have no other choice

ほかに選択肢がないために、何かをする

（最後の手段として）〜に訴える

例 Protesters may **resort to** violence if peaceful protests do not give the results they desire.

平和的な抗議活動が望む結果をもたらさない場合、抗議者たちは暴力に訴えるかもしれない。

321

yield to
《yield to 事物》

to agree to do something you were trying to avoid

避けようとしていたことをすることに同意する

〜に屈する

例 She finally **yielded to** temptation and ate one of the cookies.

彼女はついに誘惑に負けて、クッキーを1枚食べてしまった。

322

fit in with
《fit in with 人・事物》

to be accepted in a particular situation, place, or group

特定の状況、場所、またはグループにおいて受け入れられる

〈環境など〉に溶け込む、なじむ

例 Angelica has never really **fit in with** the popular crowd at school.

アンジェリカは、学校の人気者グループに溶け込んだことがない。

323

look in on
《look in on 人》

to make a short social visit to someone

社交目的で誰かを短時間訪問する

〈人〉のところにちょっと立ち寄る

例 Robert promised he'd **look in on** his mother to make sure she was all right.

ロバートは母親が元気か確認しに、彼女のところに立ち寄ると約束した。

□□□ 324

set about
《set about (*doing*) 事物》

to start doing something

例 They **set about** the task of cleaning the entire house.

〜をし始める、
〜に取りかかる

何かをし始める

彼らは家中を掃除する作業に
取りかかった。

□□□ 325

set in
《set in》

to start and be likely to continue

例 The cold weather seems to be **setting in** early this year.

〈病気・不快な天候など
が〉始まる、到来する

始まり、続きそうだ

今年は寒さが早く到来するようだ。

□□□ 326

take apart
《take 事物 apart / take apart 事物》

**to separate something into all of its
different pieces**

≒ dismantle

⇔ put together

例 Nathan decided to **take apart** his models and put
them back together again.

〈機械など〉を分解する

327句

何かをすべての異なる部分
に分ける

ネイサンは自分の模型を分解
して、もう一度組み立て直すこ
とにした。

□□□ 327

switch off
《switch 事物 off / switch off 事物》

**to turn off something by using a button or
switch**

例 All of the lights in the studio need to be **switched off**
before we leave.

〜のスイッチを切る、
〈電気など〉を消す

ボタンやスイッチを使って
何かを消す

スタジオの照明は、帰る前にす
べて消さなければならない。

cut down
《cut 事物 down / cut down 事物》

〈木〉を切り倒す

① to make something fall by cutting through the bottom of it

下の部分を切って何かを倒す

例 Ellen spent the afternoon **cutting down** trees in the forest.

エレンは午後、森の中で木を切り倒して過ごした。

〜の量を減らす、
〜を切り詰める

② to make the amount of something decrease

何かの量を減らす

例 The new train line will **cut down** my commuting time by over 30 minutes.

新しい路線のおかげで私の通勤時間は30分以上短縮される。

decide on
《decide on 事物》

（選択肢から）〜に決定する、〜を選ぶ

to choose something after considering multiple options

複数の選択肢を考慮したうえで何かを選択する

例 After thinking long and hard, she finally **decided on** the cheesecake.

彼女はじっくり考えた後、最終的にチーズケーキに決めた。

sign up for
《sign up for 事物》

〜に登録する

to put your name on a list to take part in something

何かに参加するために、リストに自分の名前を載せる

例 Clarissa **signed up for** volleyball tryouts when she entered junior high school.

クラリッサは中学校に入学したとき、バレーボールの入部テストを申し込んだ。

turn out
《turn out (to be)》

結局（〜と）なる、
（〜と）判明する

to be discovered to be

〜であることがわかる

ⓘ 後ろには形容詞または 事物 がくる。

例 Things will **turn out** all right in the end.

物事は最終的にうまくいくものだ。

《turn out》

（集まりなどに）繰り出す、
出かける

to attend an event

イベントに参加する

例 Thousands **turned out** for the charity concert last weekend.

先週末のチャリティーコンサートには何千人もの人々が集まった。

《turn 事物 out / turn out 事物》

331句

〈電灯など〉を消す、
〜のスイッチを切る

① to make a light go off using a button, switch, etc.

ボタンやスイッチなどを使って明かりを消す

例 He **turned out** the light before closing his eyes and going to sleep.

彼は目を閉じて眠りにつく前に、電気を消した。

〜を作り出す、生産する

② to produce something

何かを生産する

例 The car factory **turns out** hundreds of cars per week.

その自動車工場は、週に何百台もの車を生産している。

□□□ **332**

call off
《call 事物 off / call off 事物》

〜を中止する

to stop something that was planned, such as an event

イベントなど、予定されていたことをやめる

≒ cancel

例 They had to **call off** the fireworks show because of the approaching typhoon.

台風が接近しているため、彼らは花火大会を中止にしなければならなかった。

□□□ **333**

date back to
《date back to 事物》

〈ある時代〉にさかのぼる

to have existed since a specific time in the past

過去の特定の時点から存在している

例 The vase **dates back to** the Middle Ages.

その花瓶は中世にさかのぼる。

□□□ **334**

look on
《look on》

傍観する

to watch something without becoming involved

関与せずに何かを見る

ⓘ onlooker（傍観者）という語も覚えておこう。

例 Everyone merely **looked on** as the two people continued to fight.

2人がけんかし続けるのを、みんなはただ傍観していた。

《look on 人・事物 (as 人・事物)》

〜を…と見なす

to consider someone or something in a specific way

誰かまたは何かを特定の仕方で見なす

例 He **looks on** his boss as a good friend as well.

彼は上司のことを親友とも思っている。

get into
《get into 事物》

～の中に入る

---

① to enter a place, especially when doing so is difficult

特にそうするのが難しい場合に、ある場所に入る

ⓘ「（列車などが）～に到着する」という意味もある。

例 They couldn't **get into** the room because the door was locked.

ドアに鍵がかかっていて、彼らは部屋に入れなかった。

〈よくない事柄〉に巻き込まれる

② to start to be involved in doing something

何かをすることに関わり始める

例 She started to **get into** trouble at school.

彼女は学校で問題に巻き込まれ始めた。 335句

～を（なんとか）身に着ける、着る

③ to put on a piece of clothing with difficulty

苦労して服を身に着ける

例 He couldn't **get into** his suit because he'd gained a lot of weight over the summer.

彼は夏の間にかなり体重が増えたので、スーツが入らなかった。

～に興味を持つ、はまる

④ to start to be interested in something and enjoy it

何かに興味を持って楽しみ始める

例 Parker first **got into** trading cards when he was in elementary school.

パーカーは、小学生のときに初めてトレーディングカードにはまった。

run through
《run through 事物》

① to repeat something to practice it

例 Let's **run through** this piece one more time to make sure you've really got it.

（本番前に）〜を練習
[リハーサル]する

練習するために何かを繰り返す

ちゃんとできるように、この曲をもう1度リハーサルしましょう。

② to spend a lot of money quickly and carelessly

例 Bernie **ran through** all his savings buying expensive furniture for his new apartment.

〈金など〉を無駄遣いする、浪費する

急速かつ不注意に多額のお金を使う

バーニーは、新しいアパート用の高価な家具を買って貯金を使い果たした。

stick to
《stick to 事物》

① to continue doing or using something without wanting to change to something else

例 Let's just **stick to** the plan.

〜し続ける、
〜を使い続ける

何かほかのものに変えようとせず、何かをしたり使ったりし続ける

計画どおりに続けましょう。

② to not change your decisions or beliefs

例 **Stick to** your principles and never forget who you are.

〈決定・信念など〉を曲げない、貫く

決断や信念を変えない

自分の信念を貫き、自分が何者であるかを決して忘れないように。

□□□ 338

show off
《show off》

to try to impress someone with your abilities, possessions, etc.

見栄を張る、いきがる

自分の能力や所有物などで誰かを感心させようとする

例 Sydney couldn't resist **showing off** on the basketball court.

シドニーは、バスケットボールのコートでどうしても目立ちたがった。

《show 事物 off / show off 事物》

〈持ち物・才能など〉を見せびらかす、ひけらかす

to show others someone or something that you are proud of

自分が誇りに思っている誰かや何かを他人に見せる

例 He smiled, **showing off** his straight teeth.

彼は微笑み、並びのよい歯をのぞかせた。

339句

□□□ 339

show up
《show up》

（約束どおりに）現れる、来る

① to arrive at a place you have agreed to be at to meet someone or do something

誰かに会ったり何かをしたりするために、行くことに同意した場所に到着する

例 She may have **showed up** late, but at least she came.

彼女が現れたのは遅かったかもしれないが、少なくとも来てはくれた。

際立つ、よく見える

② to be able or easy to be seen or noticed

見られたり気づかれたりすることが可能または容易な

例 We changed the color of the logo so that it would **show up** better on marketing materials.

私たちはマーケティング資料でよりよく見えるように、ロゴの色を変更した。

□□□ **340**

go on to *do*
《go on to *do*》

続いて今度は〜する

to do something after you have finished doing something else

何かほかのことをやり終えた後に何かをする

例 After starting out as a junior recruiter, she **went on to** head her own recruitment firm.

彼女はジュニアリクルーターとしてキャリアを始め、のちに自らの人材会社の代表となった。

□□□ **341**

fill out
《fill 事物 out / fill out 事物》

〈書類など〉に必要事項を記入する

to complete a form by writing all the necessary information on it

必要な情報をすべて書き込んで用紙を完成させる

≒ fill in

例 Please **fill out** all of your personal details here.

ここに個人情報をすべて記入してください。

□□□ **342**

give away
《give 事物 away / give away 事物》

〜をただでやる

① to give something as a present instead of selling it

何かを売るのではなくプレゼントする

≒ donate

例 We're **giving away** free concert tickets to the first 10 callers.

お電話くださった先着10名様にコンサートの無料招待券を差し上げます。

〈秘密など〉をもらす

② to tell someone something that should have been a secret

秘密のはずだったことを誰かに話す

例 Sue didn't mean to **give away** your secret.

スーはあなたの秘密をもらすつもりではなかった。

□□□ **343**

devote to
《devote 事物 to 事物》

~を…にささげる

to give time or attention to something

何かに時間を割いたり注意を向けたりする

例 Thomas **devoted** his whole life **to** studying butterflies.

トーマスは蝶の研究に一生をささげた。

□□□ **344**

end in
《end in 事物》

結局~に終わる

to have something as a result

結果として何かを得る

例 Quite a few of Shakespeare's plays **end in** tragedy.

シェイクスピアの戯曲の中には、悲劇で終わるものがかなりある。

346句

□□□ **345**

leave out
《leave 人・事物 out / leave out 人・事物》

〈人・名前など〉を除外する;〈言葉・文字など〉を省く

to not include someone or something

誰かまたは何かを含めない

例 Harris **left out** the peanuts in the recipe because he's allergic.

ハリスはアレルギーがあるので、そのレシピからピーナッツを除いた。

□□□ **346**

consist in
《consist in 事物》

~にある、存在する

to have something as an important part of something

何かを何かの重要な部分とする

例 Happiness doesn't **consist in** how much money or stuff you have.

幸せは、お金やものをどれだけ持っているかにあるのではない。

□□□ **347**

drop out
《drop out》

① to stop being part of something

何かの一部であることをやめる

脱退する、引退する

ⓘ dropout（脱退者、中途退学者）という語も覚えておこう。

例 Ally **dropped out** of the volleyball team after she injured her leg.

アリーは脚をけがした後、バレーボールチームを脱退した。

退学する

② to leave school without completing your studies

学業を修了せずに学校を去る

例 Wesley **dropped out** of school when he was 16.

ウェズリーは16歳のときに学校を中退した。

□□□ **348**

eat up
《eat 事物 up / eat up 事物》

① to eat all of something

何かを全部食べる

～を食べ尽くす

ⓘ「食べ物を食べ尽くす」という自動詞の使い方もある。

例 Isabella **ate up** all the cookies in front of her.

イザベラは目の前のクッキーを全部食べ尽くした。

〈時間・燃料など〉を使い果たす

② to use up time or resources

時間や資源を使い果たす

例 The meeting **ate up** so much time that I didn't get anything done the whole afternoon.

会議でひどく時間を食ってしまい、午後は何もできなかった。

□□□ 349

enter into
《enter into 事物》

〈仕事・交渉など〉を始める、〈問題など〉を扱う

① to start something or become involved in it

何かを始める、またはそれに関与する

例 She does her best to never **enter into** arguments with people.

彼女はできる限り人と口論にならないように気をつけている。

〈協約など〉を結ぶ

② to make an official agreement about something

何かについて正式な合意をする

例 We are happy to announce that we've **entered into** a partnership with Westfield Cheese Company.

弊社がウェストフィールド・チーズ・カンパニーとパートナーシップを結んだことをお知らせします。

350句

〈議論・考察など〉に入ってくる、含まれる

③ to have an influence on something

何かに影響を与える

例 Money never **enters into** the choices he makes.

彼がする選択に、お金はまったく関係ない。

□□□ 350

look to
《look to 事物》

〜について考える、注意を払う

to pay attention to something, especially to improve it

特に改善するために、何かに注意を払う

ⓘ look to forも参照。

例 You must **look to** ways to improve yourself without help from others.

他人の助けを借りずに自分を高める方法について考えなさい。

351

relieve of
《relieve 人 of 事物》

〈人〉から～を取り除い
てやる

① to take something that someone is struggling with from them

誰かが苦労しているものを
その人から取り去る

例 The manager hired a second accountant to help **relieve** her **of** some of her tasks.

部長は彼女の仕事の一部を軽
減するために、2人目の会計
士を雇った。

～から〈人〉を解雇する

② to remove someone from a position because they have done something wrong

誰かが何か間違ったことを
したために、その人を地位
から外す

例 Ms. Meyers was **relieved of** her position after it was discovered she was stealing.

マイヤーズさんは盗みを働い
ていたことが発覚し、その職を
解かれた。

352

see to
《see to 事物》

～の手はずを整える、
～に処置を施す

to deal with something

何かを処理する

例 My assistant Daniel will **see to** the flight and hotel arrangements.

アシスタントのダニエルが飛行
機とホテルの手配を行います。

353

specialize in
《specialize in 事物》

～を専門にする

to focus your business, studies, etc. on a specific area

ビジネス、研究などを特定
の分野に集中させる

例 Dr. Han **specializes in** treating cancer.

ハン医師は、がんの治療を専
門にしている。

□□□ 354

sum up
《sum 事物 up / sum up 事物》

～を要約する、
かいつまんで話す

to briefly state the main points of something

何かの要点を簡潔に述べる

≒ summarize

ⓘ 自動詞の使い方もある。

例 You **summed up** the key points perfectly.

あなたは要点を完ぺきにまとめました。

□□□ 355

rest with
《rest with 人・事物》

～次第である、
～に責任がある

to be the responsibility of someone or something

誰かまたは何かの責任である

356句

例 All final decisions regarding this matter **rest with** the CEO.

この件に関する最終決定はすべて、CEOに委ねられている。

□□□ 356

break out
《break out》

〈火事・戦争・伝染病などが〉急に始まる、勃発する

① to start suddenly

突然始まる

ⓘ outbreak（勃発）という語も覚えておこう。

例 When the war **broke out**, thousands of people's lives changed completely overnight.

戦争が始まると、一夜にして何千人もの人々の生活が一変してしまった。

（場所から）脱出する

② to escape from a place or situation

ある場所や状況から逃れる

ⓘ breakout（脱獄、脱走）という語も覚えておこう。

例 The man **broke out** of prison after only being there for a few months.

その男は数か月間そこにいただけで、刑務所から脱走した。

lay aside
《lay 事物 aside / lay aside 事物》

〜を脇へ[下へ]置く、脇へやる

---

① **to put something to the side**

何かを脇に置く

≒ put aside

例 Laurel **laid aside** her knitting to take a look out the window.

ローレルは窓の外を見るために、編み物を脇に置いた。

〈金など〉を取っておく

② **to keep something to use at a later time**

後日使うために何かを取っておく

≒ put aside

例 He **lays aside** fifty percent of his tips.

彼はチップの半分を取っておいている。

bring up
《bring 人 up / bring up 人》

〈子ども〉を育てる

---

to take care of a child and teach them how to act until they are grown up

子どもの世話をし、大人になるまで行動の仕方を教える

≒ raise

例 Clark was **brought up** by his aunt and uncle.

クラークはおばとおじに育てられた。

《bring 事物 up / bring up 事物》

〈問題・話題など〉を持ち出す

---

to mention something or start to talk about it

何かに言及する、またはそれについて話し始める

≒ raise

例 Please don't **bring up** the dinner, as the fact that we're going is meant to be a surprise.

ディナーに行くというのはサプライズのつもりなので、その話は持ち出さないでね。

□□□ 359

refrain from

~を差し控える、堪える

《refrain from 事物 / refrain from *doing*》

to stop yourself from doing something that you want to do

自分がしたい何かをするの をやめる

例 We ask that all guests **refrain from** talking on their cell phones for the duration of the event.

イベント中は携帯電話での通 話はお控えいただきますよう、 ご来場の皆さまにお願い申し 上げます。

□□□ 360

hang on

（ものに）しっかりつかま る、しがみつく

《hang on (to 事物)》

to hold something tightly

何かを強く握る

360句

例 Walter **hung on** to his bag tightly as he made his way through the crowd.

ウォルターはかばんをしっかり 抱えて、人混みの中を進んだ。

《hang on》

（苦境を）持ちこたえる

to continue doing something despite being in a difficult situation

困難な状況にあるにもかか わらず、何かをし続ける

例 The team managed to **hang on** until the end and win the game.

そのチームは最後まで粘って、 何とか試合に勝った。

《hang on 事物》

~次第である、 ~にかかっている

to depend on something

何か次第である

例 The entire match **hangs on** the outcome of this penalty kick.

試合の行方はこのPKの結果に かかっている。

□□□ **361**

come to
《come to》

to become conscious again
意識を取り戻す

再び意識のある状態になる

≒ come around
⇔ faint, pass out

例 When she **came to**, she was lying in a hospital bed.
彼女は気がつくと、病院のベッドに横たわっていた。

《come to 事物》
合計〜になる

① to add up to a total amount
合計して総量になる

例 The total for your order **comes to** $4.51.
ご注文の合計は、4.51ドルになります。

〈ある状態〉になる、達する

② to develop so that a bad situation exists
悪い状況が存在するような仕方で展開する

例 Nobody ever thought it would **come to** this.
こんなことになるとは、誰も思ってもみなかった。

《come to 人》
〈考えなどが〉〈人〉に浮かぶ

to enter someone's mind
誰かの心に入る

例 The answer **came to** her suddenly in the shower.
その答えは、彼女がシャワーを浴びているときに突然思い浮かんだ。

□□□ 362

dispose of
《dispose of 事物》

〈不要なもの・やっかいなもの〉を処分する

① to throw something away

何かを捨てる

例 Needles must be **disposed of** carefully so they don't harm anyone.

誰にも害を与えないように、針は気をつけて処分しなければならない。

〈問題など〉を処理する

② to deal with and finish something

何かに対処して終わらせる

例 And with that, it seems we've **disposed of** most of your arguments.

これで、私たちはあなたの論点のほとんどに対処したようです。

363句

□□□ 363

dry up
《dry up》

完全に乾く；干上がる

① to become completely dry

完全に乾燥する

例 There hasn't been rain in weeks, so the river **dried up**.

何週間も雨が降っていないので、川が干上がった。

なくなる、尽きる

② to come to an end and have no more available

終わりが来て、もはや手に入らない

例 Work soon **dried up**, and David had to return to his hometown.

仕事はすぐになくなり、デイヴィッドは故郷に帰らなければならなかった。

章末ボキャブラリーチェック

次の語義が表す英熟語を答えてください。

語義	解答	連番
❶ to repeat something to practice it	run through	336
❷ to not change your decisions or beliefs	stick to	337
❸ to accept something or someone that is not pleasant	put up with	318
❹ to leave school without completing your studies	drop out	347
❺ to deal with and finish something	dispose of	362
❻ to stop something that was planned, such as an event	call off	332
❼ to focus your business, studies, etc. on a specific area	specialize in	353
❽ to briefly state the main points of something	sum up	354
❾ to mention something or start to talk about it	bring up	358
❿ to do something after you have finished doing something else	go on to *do*	340
⓫ to finish doing something	get through with	315
⓬ to stop yourself from doing something that you want to do	refrain from	359
⓭ to choose something after considering multiple options	decide on	329
⓮ to remove someone from a position because they have done something wrong	relieve of	351
⓯ to depend on something	hang on	360
⓰ to be accepted in a particular situation, place, or group	fit in with	322
⓱ to have an influence on something	enter into	349
⓲ to have something as a result	end in	344
⓳ to think of an idea or answer to something	come up with	317
⓴ to produce something	turn out	331

語義	解答	連番
㉑ to agree to do something you were trying to avoid	y i e l d t o	321
㉒ to put something to the side	l a y a s i d e	357
㉓ to watch something without becoming involved	l o o k o n	334
㉔ to give something to someone, especially after receiving it from someone else or using it yourself	p a s s o n t o	316
㉕ to take care of a child and teach them how to act until they are grown up	b r i n g u p	358
㉖ to start something or become involved in it	e n t e r i n t o	349
㉗ to become conscious again	c o m e t o	361
㉘ to use up time or resources	e a t u p	348
㉙ to start to be interested in something and enjoy it	g e t i n t o	335
㉚ to show others someone or something that you are proud of	s h o w o f f	338
㉛ to escape from a place or situation	b r e a k o u t	356
㉜ to make the amount of something decrease	c u t d o w n	328
㉝ to hold something tightly	h a n g o n	360
㉞ to become completely dry	d r y u p	363
㉟ to make a short social visit to someone	l o o k i n o n	323
㊱ to continue doing something despite being in a difficult situation	h a n g o n	360
㊲ to turn off something by using a button or switch	s w i t c h o f f	327
㊳ to be discovered to be	t u r n o u t	331
㊴ to make an official agreement about something	e n t e r i n t o	349
㊵ to make something fall by cutting through the bottom of it	c u t d o w n	328
㊶ to keep something to use at a later time	l a y a s i d e	357
㊷ to spend a lot of money quickly and carelessly	r u n t h r o u g h	336
㊸ to take something away from someone or something, or prevent them from getting it	d e p r i v e o f	313
㊹ to put on a piece of clothing with difficulty	g e t i n t o	335

45 to continue doing or using something without wanting to change to something else — stick to — 337

46 to give time or attention to something — devote to — 343

47 to consider someone or something in a specific way — look on — 334

48 to eat all of something — eat up — 348

49 to arrive at a place you have agreed to be at to meet someone or do something — show up — 339

50 to make a light go off using a button, switch, etc. — turn out — 331

51 to start doing something — set about — 324

52 to help or speak to someone, especially a customer or guest — attend to — 319

53 to be the responsibility of someone or something — rest with — 355

54 to start to be involved in doing something — get into — 335

55 to give something as a present instead of selling it — give away — 342

56 to enter someone's mind — come to — 361

57 to give most of your time and energy to someone or something — devote yourself to — 314

58 to attend an event — turn out — 331

59 to put your name on a list to take part in something — sign up for — 330

60 to do something because you have no other choice — resort to — 320

61 to have something as an important part of something — consist in — 346

62 to not include someone or something — leave out — 345

63 to come to an end and have no more available — dry up — 363

64 to deal with something — attend to — 319

65 to try to impress someone with your abilities, possessions, etc. — show off — 338

66 to pay attention to something, especially to improve it — look to — 350

67 to start suddenly — break out — 356

68 to develop so that a bad situation exists — come to — 361

語義	解答	連番
⑥⑨ to deal with something	s̲e̲e̲ t̲o̲	352
⑦⓪ to stop being part of something	d̲r̲o̲p̲ o̲u̲t̲	347
⑦① to separate something into all of its different pieces	t̲a̲k̲e̲ a̲p̲a̲r̲t̲	326
⑦② to take something that someone is struggling with from them	r̲e̲l̲i̲e̲v̲e̲ o̲f̲	351
⑦③ to add up to a total amount	c̲o̲m̲e̲ t̲o̲	361
⑦④ to start and be likely to continue	s̲e̲t̲ i̲n̲	325
⑦⑤ to throw something away	d̲i̲s̲p̲o̲s̲e̲ o̲f̲	362
⑦⑥ to be able or easy to be seen or noticed	s̲h̲o̲w̲ u̲p̲	339
⑦⑦ to enter a place, especially when doing so is difficult	g̲e̲t̲ i̲n̲t̲o̲	335
⑦⑧ to complete a form by writing all the necessary information on it	f̲i̲l̲l̲ o̲u̲t̲	341
⑦⑨ to tell someone something that should have been a secret	g̲i̲v̲e̲ a̲w̲a̲y̲	342
⑧⓪ to have existed since a specific time in the past	d̲a̲t̲e̲ b̲a̲c̲k̲ t̲o̲	333

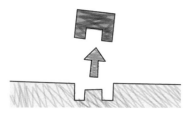

SET OFF (→440)

setは「〜を置く」という意味の動詞
ですが、単に「ポンと置く」イメージ
のputと違い、「慎重に置く、設定
する」というニュアンスの単語です。
一方、offは分離を意味する副詞で、
set offは「設定されたものが、その
状態を離れてスタートする」イメージを表します。そこから、「（計画された旅
行に）出発する」「〈爆弾など〉を爆発させる」「〈警報装置など〉を作動させ
始める」といった意味が出てきます。より抽象的に〈出来事など〉を引き起こ
す、始めさせる」という意味も表します。

①（旅行などに）出発する
They packed up their car and **set off** on a cross-country road trip.
（彼らは車に荷物を積み込み、全国旅行に出発した。）

②〈出来事など〉を引き起こす、始めさせる
Enrolling in the tango class **set off** a series of events that ended with him
living in Brazil.
（タンゴのクラスに参加したことがきっかけでいろいろなことが起こり、結局彼はブラ
ジルに住むことになった。）

③〈爆弾など〉を爆発させる
Construction companies must follow strict regulations when **setting off**
any kind of explosives.
（建設会社はどんな種類の爆薬を爆発させるときにも、厳しい規則に従わなければな
らない。）

④〈警報装置など〉を作動させ始める
The neighborhood cats are always **setting off** the motion sensor lights.
（近所の猫たちはいつも人感センサーライトを作動させている。）

Stage 7

Where there's a will, there's a way.
志あるところに道あり。

□□□ 364

bring out
《bring 事物 out / bring out 事物》

〈本・商品など〉を新しく
出す

① to make something that will be sold to others

他人に売るものを作る

例 Her favorite band is **bringing out** a new album next week.

彼女の好きなバンドが来週、新しいアルバムを出す。

〈資質・特徴など〉を引き
出す；～を際立たせる

② to make something easier to notice

何かを気づきやすくする

例 The salt really **brings out** the flavor of the vegetables in this soup.

塩は、このスープの野菜の風味をとても引き立てている。

□□□ 365

keep to
《keep to 事物》

〈約束など〉を守る；
〈規則など〉に従う

① to do what you have agreed to do or what is required by law

すると同意したことや法律で定められていることを行う

≒ obey

例 **Keep to** the speed limit, and the police won't bother you.

制限速度を守りなさい。そうすれば警察に煩わされることはないから。

〈道・場所など〉から離
れない

② to avoid leaving a certain place

ある場所から離れるのを避ける

ⓘ 比喩的に「〈話題など〉から逸脱しない」という意味もある。

例 If you **keep to** this path, you'll reach the lake soon.

この道を外れずに行けば、すぐに湖に着きますよ。

□□□ 366

feed on
《feed on 事物》

〈動物が〉～を食べて生きる

to eat something

何かを食べる

≒ feed off

例 Some bears **feed on** both plants and small animals.

クマの中には植物と小動物の両方をえさにするものがいる。

□□□ 367

leave off
《leave off》

やめる

to stop something, such as a story or a conversation, especially before it is finished

物語や会話など何かを、特にそれが終了する前にやめる

368句

(i) leave off *doing*（～し終える）の形で使われることもある。

例 Where did we **leave off** at the end of the last meeting?

前回のミーティングは、どこで終わったんでしたっけ。

□□□ 368

allow for
《allow for 人・事物》

～を考慮に入れる

to consider someone or something when making a calculation

計算をするときに誰かまたは何かを考慮する

例 Even **allowing for** inflation, the cost of tickets has doubled.

インフレを考慮しても、チケットの値段は2倍になっている。

《allow for 事物》

～を可能にする

to make something possible

何かを可能にする

例 The game's complex storyline **allows for** many paths to victory.

そのゲームの複雑なストーリー展開は、勝利への多くの道を可能にしている。

□□□ 369

speak out against
《speak out against 事物》

〜への反対を表明する

to say your opinion to oppose something publicly

何かに公式に反対するために、自分の意見を言う

例 Many students have **spoken out against** the strict dress code at the school.

多くの生徒が学校の厳しい服装規定に反対を表明している。

□□□ 370

sell out
《sell out》

売り切る、売り尽くす

① to sell all of the available items, tickets, etc. and have none remaining

販売可能な商品、チケットなどをすべて販売し、残りがなくなる

例 Unfortunately, it seems that we've **sold out** of your size.

残念ながら、お求めのサイズは売り切れのようです。

〈切符などが〉売り切れる

② to be completely sold

完全に売却される

例 All of the shows on her North American tour **sold out** within minutes.

彼女の北米ツアーの公演はすべて、数分で完売した。

信念などを曲げる

③ to change or give up your beliefs, especially for some advantage

特に何らかの利益のために、自分の信念を変える、または捨てる

例 Although it's his most popular album to date, some of his oldest fans think he has **sold out**.

これまでで最も人気のあるアルバムだが、古くからのファンの中には彼が信念を曲げたと考える人もいる。

□□□ 371

go about
《go about 事物》

〈仕事・問題など〉に取りかかる、着手する

① to start doing something

何かを始める

例 Kara wants to become fluent in Mandarin, but she doesn't know the best way to **go about** it.

カーラは北京語を流ちょうに話せるようになりたいと思っているが、一番いい始め方がわからない。

〈仕事など〉を行う、こなす

② to do something in the usual way

いつもの仕方で何かをする

例 He **went about** his business as usual.

彼はいつものように仕事をこなした。

372句

□□□ 372

feel for
《feel for 事物》

～を手探りで探す

to search for something when you cannot see

見えない中で何かを探す

例 She **felt for** her glasses in the dark.

彼女は暗闇の中、手探りで眼鏡を探した。

《feel for 人》

〈人〉に同情する、共鳴する

to feel sympathy for someone

誰かに同情する

例 I **feel for** you. I was devastated when my trip to Thailand got canceled last year.

気持ちはよくわかるよ。私も去年、タイ旅行が中止になったときは大ショックだったから。

□□□ 373

give off
《give off 事物》

〈におい・光など〉を放つ

---

to produce a smell, light, etc.

におい、光などを発生させる

例 The lamp in the corner of the room **gives off** a soft and pale light.

部屋の隅にあるランプは柔らかく淡い光を放っている。

□□□ 374

make out
《make 事物 out / make out 事物》

〈書類など〉を（正式に）作成する、書く

---

① to write information on a check, document, etc.

小切手、書類などに情報を書く

≒ write out

例 Please **make out** the check to my sister-in-law.

小切手は義姉宛てに出してください。

〜を理解する、〜がわかる

② to understand something

何かを理解する

例 I can't **make out** why he's angry with me.

なぜ彼が私に腹を立てているのかわからない。

〜を（なんとか）見分ける；〜を判読する

③ to just be able to see or hear someone or something

誰かまたは何かをなんとか見たり聞いたりすることができる

例 Sorry, we can't **make out** what you're saying.

すみません、おっしゃっていることが聞き取れません。

□□□ 375

back up
《back up》

後退する

to move backwards

後方に移動する

例 The van slowly **backed up** to the front door.

バンは玄関までゆっくりとバックした。

《back 人·事物 up / back up 人·事物》

〜を支持する、支援する

to give support or help to someone or something

誰かまたは何かにサポートや援助を与える

例 Don't worry, we'll **back** you **up** if it comes to that.

心配しないでください。必要なときは、私たちが支援しますから。

376句

《back 事物 up / back up 事物》

〈データなど〉のバックアップをとる

to make a copy of something stored on a computer

コンピュータに保存されているもののコピーを作成する

(i) backup（バックアップ）という語も覚えておこう。

例 You should regularly **back up** all important files on your computer.

コンピュータの重要なファイルはすべて、定期的にバックアップをとっておいたほうがいいですよ。

□□□ 376

object to
《object to 事物》

〜に反対する

to say that you do not agree with something

何かに同意しないと言う

例 Many parents **object to** the inclusion of sex education in school curriculums.

多くの親は、学校のカリキュラムに性教育を含めることに反対している。

□ □ □ **377**

bring down

《bring 人・事物 down / bring down 人・事物》

～を倒す

---

to make someone or something fall down

誰かまたは何かが倒れるようにする

[例] They finally managed to **bring down** the player right before he scored.

彼らは得点される直前にようやくその選手を倒すことができた。

《bring 事物 down / bring down 事物》

〈値段〉を下げる;〈水準・率など〉を低くする

---

to make something be lower

何かを低くする

[例] The bank is hoping to help the economy by **bringing down** interest rates.

銀行は、金利を下げることで経済を助けることを望んでいる。

《bring 人 down / bring down 人》

〈人〉を意気消沈させる

---

to cause someone to become sad, lose confidence, etc.

誰かを悲しませたり、自信をなくさせたりする

[例] Don't let the things other people tell you **bring** you **down**.

ほかの人に言われたことで、落ち込まないでください。

□ □ □ **378**

long for

《long for 事物》

～を切望する

---

to want something a lot, especially when it seems unlikely to happen soon

特にすぐにはかないそうにないときに、何かをひどく欲しがる

≒ yearn for

[例] He **longs for** the day his favorite band will finally perform a show in his city.

彼は、好きなバンドが自分の住む市でついに公演する日を待ちわびている。

□□□ 379

insist on

《insist on 事物》

〜を要求する

① to demand something and not be persuaded to accept anything else

何かを要求し、それ以外の ものを受け入れるようには 説得されない

例 The couple **insisted on** a refund after their meal was ruined.

カップルは食事が台無しにな ると、返金を要求した。

〜を主張する

② to say strongly and often that something is true, even if others do not think so

ほかの人がそうは思わなく ても、何かが真実であると 強く頻繁に言う

380句

例 Marc **insisted on** his innocence, despite the evidence against him.

マークは自分に不利な証拠が あるにもかかわらず、無実を主 張した。

《insist on *doing*》

（迷惑を顧みず）〜し続 ける

to keep doing something even though someone else might think it is inconvenient or annoying

ほかの誰かが厄介だと思っ たり迷惑だと思ったりして も、何かをし続ける

例 Grace **insisted on** listening to her music at max volume even though her parents hated it.

グレースは、両親が嫌がってい るのに音楽を最大音量で聞き 続けた。

□□□ 380

give yourself up to

《give yourself up to 事物》

〈感情など〉に身を任せる

to allow yourself to feel or show an emotion completely

感情を完全に感じたり、表 現したりすることを自分に 許す

例 It's OK to **give yourself up to** your emotions sometimes.

時には感情に身を任せてもい いんですよ。

□□□ 381

call for
《call for 事物》

① to publicly ask for something

〜を声を上げて求める、要求する

公に何かを求める

例 Environmental groups are **calling for** stronger policies against fossil fuels.

環境保護団体は、化石燃料に対するより強力な政策を要求している。

〜を必要とする

② to require or demand something

何かを必要とする、または要求する

例 I'm so happy you got the job! This **calls for** a celebration.

仕事が決まってよかったね！お祝いしなきゃ。

□□□ 382

hang around
《hang around 事物》

〜のあたりをぶらつく、たむろする

to spend time somewhere waiting or doing nothing

待ちながら、または何もするでもなく、どこかで時間を過ごす

≒ hang out

ⓘ 「ぶらつく」という自動詞の使い方もある。hang around with も参照。

例 The teens spent their weekends **hanging around** the mall.

その10代の若者たちは、週末になるとショッピングモールでぶらぶらして過ごした。

□□□ 383

lose yourself in
《lose yourself in 事物》

〜に夢中になる

to give all your attention to something

すべての注意を何かに向ける

例 There is nothing better than **losing yourself in** a book.

本に夢中になることほど、素晴らしいことはない。

□□□ 384

run down
《run 人・事物 down / run down 人・事物》

〈車・運転手が〉〈人・動物など〉をはねる

① **to hit someone or something with a vehicle and injure or kill them, especially intentionally**

特に故意に誰かまたは何かに車をぶつけ、けがをさせたり殺したりする

例 She was arrested for attempted murder after she tried to **run down** her ex-boyfriend with her car.

彼女は元カレを車でひき殺そうとし、殺人未遂で逮捕された。

〈考え・人など〉をこき下ろす、けなす

385句

② **to criticize someone or something unkindly**

誰かまたは何かを思いやりなく批判する

≒ put down

例 Why are you with her if she's always **running** you **down**?

いつもけなされているのに、どうして彼女と一緒にいるの?

《run down》

〈機械などが〉止まる、〈電池が〉切れる

to lose power or stop working

力を失う、または動作を停止する

例 The car battery has finally **run down**.

その車のバッテリーは、とうとう切れた。

□□□ 385

talk out of *doing*
《talk 人 out of *doing*》

〈人〉を説得して〜するのをやめさせる

to convince someone not to do something

何かをしないよう誰かを説得する

⇔ talk into *doing*

例 Luckily she was able to **talk** her brother **out of** entering the competition.

幸い、彼女は弟を説得してその大会に出るのをやめさせることができた。

□□□ 386

surrender to
《surrender to 人》

〈人〉に降伏する、
降参する

to admit you have lost and want to stop fighting

負けたことを認め、戦いを
やめることを望む

≒ give in to

例 The rebels had to **surrender to** the government.

反乱軍は政府に降伏しなけれ
ばならなかった。

《surrender to 事物》

〈感情・癖など〉に身を
委ねる

to let yourself be controlled or influenced by something

何かに支配されたり、影響
されたりするままにする

例 Frank finally **surrendered to** sleep.

フランクは睡魔に勝てずついに
眠りに落ちた。

□□□ 387

think out
《think 事物 out / think out 事物》

〜についてよく考える、
熟慮する

to consider something carefully

何かを慎重に検討する

例 She likes to **think** things **out** during her morning runs.

彼女は、朝のランニング中に考
え事をするのが好きだ。

□□□ 388

try out
《try 人・事物 out / try out 人・事物》

〈人・方法・装置など〉を
（機能するか）テストする

to test someone or something to see if they are suitable for something

誰かまたは何かが何かに適
しているかどうかを確認す
るためにテストする

例 Lawrence went to the store to **try out** the computer he was thinking about buying.

ローレンスは、買おうと思って
いたコンピュータを試してみる
ため店に行った。

□□□ 389

hand over
《hand 人·事物 over / hand over 人·事物》

～を引き渡す、手渡す

① **to give someone or something to someone else, especially because they have asked for it or should have it**

誰かまたは何かをほかの誰かに与える。特に、その人がそれを要求した、またはそれを持つべきだという理由で

例 Cheng **handed over** his phone to the girl so that she could see the picture herself.

チェンは、少女がその写真を自分で見ることができるように、携帯電話を彼女に手渡した。

～を譲渡する

390句

② **to give someone your position or responsibilities**

誰かに自分の地位や責任を与える

例 After her retirement, Claire **handed over** the family business to her daughter.

クレアは引退後、家業を娘に譲った。

□□□ 390

act on
《act on 事物》

～に基づいて行動する

① **to take action because of advice or information**

アドバイスや情報によって行動を起こす

例 Christopher is **acting on** the advice of his lawyers.

クリストファーは弁護士の忠告に基づいて行動している。

～に作用する

② **to have an effect on something**

何かに影響を与える

例 This medicine **acts on** the immune system.

この薬は免疫系に作用する。

□□□ 391

inquire into

~を調査する

《inquire into 事物》

to ask questions in order to find out more about something

何かについてもっと知るために質問する

≒ investigate

例 The tax agent **inquired into** all of the financial dealings of her late father.

税理士は彼女の亡父の金融取引をすべて調べた。

□□□ 392

let out

~を外に出す

《let 人・事物 out / let out 人・事物》

to release someone or something

誰かまたは何かを解放する

例 Melissa always **lets** her rabbits **out** of their cage on weekends.

メリッサは毎週末、飼っているウサギをケージから外に出してやる。

《let 事物 out / let out 事物》

〈叫び声など〉を発する

to make a noise

物音を立てる

例 Carl **let out** a yell as he jumped into the lake.

カールは叫び声をあげて湖に飛び込んだ。

《let out》

〈学校などが〉終わる

to come to an end and allow people to leave

終了して、人々を帰らせる

例 School **let out** for the summer at the beginning of June.

学校は6月初めに終わり、夏休みに入った。

□□□ 393

take over

《take 事物 over / take over 事物》

〈仕事など〉を引き継ぐ

① to start doing something that someone else was doing

ほかの誰かがしていたことをやり始める

例 Can you **take over** stirring this for me while I go and check the oven?

オーブンを見にいってくる間、これをかき混ぜるのを代わってくれる?

～の支配権を握る

② to gain control of something, such as a business

ビジネスなど何かを支配する

394句

例 After she **took over** the company, profits started to increase significantly.

彼女が会社の実権を握ってから、利益が大きく伸び始めた。

□□□ 394

hold on to

《hold on to 人・事物》

～につかまっている

to hold someone or something tightly

誰かまたは何かをしっかりとつかむ

例 Make sure to **hold on to** the railing when you are walking down the stairs.

階段を下りるときは、必ず手すりにつかまってください。

《hold on to 事物》

～を手放さない

to keep something

何かを保持する

例 Remi has **held on to** her mother's old jewelry for all these years.

レミは、母親の古いジュエリーをここ何年もずっと手放さない。

☐☐☐ **395**

go together
《go together》

① to be or look good together

調和している

調和する、または似合う

例 Do you think this dress and my gold earrings will **go together**?

このドレスと私のゴールドのイヤリングは合うと思う?

---

② to exist together

一緒に起こる

一緒に存在する

≒ go hand in hand

例 Greed and wealth seem to **go together** a lot of the time.

欲と富は、しばしば相伴うようだ。

☐☐☐ **396**

spring from
《spring from 事物》

to be caused by something

〜から生じる、
〜に起因する

何かによって引き起こされる

例 Behavior **springing from** prejudices will not be tolerated here.

偏見に基づく行動は、ここでは許されない。

☐☐☐ **397**

live up to
《live up to 事物》

to do as well as other people expected

〈期待など〉に応える、
添う

ほかの人たちが期待したくらいうまくやる

例 This play has definitely **lived up to** my expectations.

この劇は間違いなく私の期待に応えてくれた。

□□□ 398

look out for
《look out for 事物》

~に気をつける、
注意する

to try to avoid something bad happening

何か悪いことが起きないようにする

≒ watch out for

例 **Look out for** spelling mistakes when submitting work professionally.

プロとして仕事を提出するときは、スペルミスに気をつけましょう。

《look out for 人》

〈人〉の世話をする、
〈人〉のことを気にかける

399句

to take care of someone so that nothing bad happens to them

誰かに悪いことが起こらないように世話をする

例 Be sure to **look out for** your little sister while you're at the park.

公園にいるときは、妹のことを気にかけるようにしてね。

□□□ 399

answer for
《answer for 事物》

~の責任を取る

to be responsible for something

何かに責任を持つ

例 You will have to **answer for** your behavior eventually.

あなたはいずれ自分の行動の責任を取らなければならないでしょう。

《answer for 人・事物》

〈人の性格・能力など〉
を保証する

to promise that someone has a certain quality or can be relied on

誰かが特定の資質を持っている、または信頼できると約束する

例 John says he can **answer for** her ability to paint portraits.

ジョンは、肖像画を描く彼女の能力は請け合うと言っている。

□□□ **400**

meet with
《meet with 事物》

〈困難など〉に遭遇する、
〜を経験する

to experience something bad

何か悪いことを経験する

例 Her brother was late arriving home, so she was worried he had **met with** an accident.

彼女は、兄の帰りが遅かったので、事故に遭ったのではないかと心配した。

《meet with 人》

〈人〉と（約束して）会う

to meet someone to discuss something

何かを話し合うために誰かに会う

例 The President **met with** her advisers to discuss climate change.

大統領は気候変動について話し合うため、顧問たちと会合を持った。

□□□ **401**

pass for
《pass for 事物》

〜として通る

to be accepted as something

何かとして受け入れられる

例 His Chinese is so good that he often **passes for** a native speaker.

彼の中国語はとても上手なので、よくネイティブと間違えられる。

□□□ **402**

break with
《break with 事物》

〈古い考えなど〉を捨てる

to stop following old beliefs and do something in a new or different way

古い信念に従うのをやめ、新しい、または異なる仕方で何かをする

例 It's time to **break with** the past and focus on the present.

過去を捨て、今に集中するときだ。

182

□□□ 403

pick up
《pick 人・事物 up / pick up 人・事物》

〜を拾い上げる、
持ち上げる

to lift someone or something

誰かまたは何かを持ち上げる

例 Augustus **picked up** his little sister and spun her around.

オーガスタスは妹を抱き上げてくるくる回した。

《pick 人 up / pick up 人》

〈人〉を（乗り物で）迎えに行く

403句

to go to a place, especially in a vehicle, to collect someone who is waiting for you

ある場所へ、特に乗り物で行き、あなたを待っている誰かを乗せる

例 Trevor **picked up** his girlfriend from work yesterday.

トレヴァーは昨日、ガールフレンドを職場に迎えに行った。

《pick 事物 up / pick up 事物》

〜を手に入れる、買う

① to buy something from a shop

店で何かを買う

例 Wendy went to the store and **picked up** some milk.

ウェンディーはその店に行って、牛乳を買った。

〈技術・知識など〉を身につける

② to learn something in an informal way

非公式な仕方で何かを学ぶ

例 She was able to **pick up** German naturally simply by living in Germany.

彼女はドイツに住んでいるだけで、自然にドイツ語を身につけることができた。

□□□ **404**

end up
《end up》

最後には（〜に）なる、
（〜で）終わる

to be in a specific situation, especially one you did not plan to be in

特定の状況、特に自分が意図
していなかった状況になる

ⓘ end up *doing*（最後には〜することになる）という形の使い方もある。

例 Sandy wasn't quite sure how she'd **ended up** at the party.

サンディーは、自分でもよくわからないうちにパーティーに来ることになっていた。

□□□ **405**

blow up
《blow up》

爆発する

① to be destroyed by an explosion

爆発によって破壊される

ⓘ「〜を爆発させる」という他動詞の使い方もある。

例 The building **blew up** and rubble flew everywhere.

その建物は爆発し、がれきがあちこちに飛び散った。

（人に）怒る、かっとなる

② to get angry with someone

誰かに腹を立てる

≒ lose your temper

例 Isaac **blew up** at his friend for using his pen.

アイザックは、友人にペンを使われてかっとなった。

《blow 事物 up / blow up 事物》

〜を膨らませる

to fill something with air

何かを空気で満たす

≒ inflate

例 Eleanor went to the shop to **blow up** her bike tires.

エレノアは、自転車のタイヤに空気を入れるためにその店に行った。

□□□ 406

break off
《break 事物 off / break off 事物》

〈会話など〉を急にやめる、中断する

① to stop talking suddenly

突然話すのをやめる

ⓘ「（会話などを）急にやめる」という自動詞の使い方もある。

例 Dustin **broke off** talking to blow his nose.

ダスティンは、話を途中で中断して鼻をかんだ。

〈関係・協定など〉を急に断つ

407句

② to end a relationship

関係を終わらせる

例 The country **broke off** relationships with its neighbor because of the war.

その国は戦争のせいで隣国との関係を断った。

《break off》

（壊れて）外れる、取れる

to become separated from something because of force

力によって何かから切り離される

ⓘ「〜を外す、取る」という他動詞の使い方もある。

例 A piece of the glacier **broke off** and created a huge splash.

氷河の一部が割れて巨大なしぶきを上げた。

□□□ 407

cut out
《cut 事物 out / cut out 事物》

〜を削除する、省略する

to leave something out of something

何かから何かを除外する

≒ omit

例 She decided to **cut out** the bit where the queen ran away from the palace.

彼女は、女王が宮殿から逃げ出した部分を省略することにした。

章末ボキャブラリーチェック

次の語義が表す英熟語を答えてください。

語義	解答	連番
❶ to make a noise	let out	392
❷ to keep something	hold on to	394
❸ to be destroyed by an explosion	blow up	405
❹ to buy something from a shop	pick up	403
❺ to make something be lower	bring down	377
❻ to take care of someone so that nothing bad happens to them	look out for	398
❼ to gain control of something, such as a business	take over	393
❽ to require or demand something	call for	381
❾ to admit you have lost and want to stop fighting	surrender to	386
❿ to spend time somewhere waiting or doing nothing	hang around	382
⓫ to search for something when you cannot see	feel for	372
⓬ to be in a specific situation, especially one you did not plan to be in	end up	404
⓭ to hit someone or something with a vehicle and injure or kill them, especially intentionally	run down	384
⓮ to change or give up your beliefs, especially for some advantage	sell out	370
⓯ to publicly ask for something	call for	381
⓰ to take action because of advice or information	act on	390
⓱ to give someone your position or responsibilities	hand over	389
⓲ to want something a lot, especially when it seems unlikely to happen soon	long for	378
⓳ to do what you have agreed to do or what is required by law	keep to	365
⓴ to meet someone to discuss something	meet with	400
㉑ to do as well as other people expected	live up to	397
㉒ to experience something bad	meet with	400

語義	解答	連番
㉓ to lose power or stop working	run down	384
㉔ to have an effect on something	act on	390
㉕ to lift someone or something	pick up	403
㉖ to start doing something that someone else was doing	take over	393
㉗ to become separated from something because of force	break off	406
㉘ to understand something	make out	374
㉙ to come to an end and allow people to leave	let out	392
㉚ to fill something with air	blow up	405
㉛ to keep doing something even though someone else might think it is inconvenient or annoying	insist on	379
㉜ to convince someone not to do something	talk out of *doing*	385
㉝ to make something easier to notice	bring out	364
㉞ to allow yourself to feel or show an emotion completely	give yourself up to	380
㉟ to produce a smell, light, etc.	give off	373
㊱ to exist together	go together	395
㊲ to be caused by something	spring from	396
㊳ to make someone or something fall down	bring down	377
㊴ to write information on a check, document, etc.	make out	374
㊵ to go to a place, especially in a vehicle, to collect someone who is waiting for you	pick up	403
㊶ to do something in the usual way	go about	371
㊷ to leave something out of something	cut out	407
㊸ to just be able to see or hear someone or something	make out	374
㊹ to give all your attention to something	lose yourself in	383
㊺ to consider someone or something when making a calculation	allow for	368
㊻ to stop talking suddenly	break off	406

語義	解答	連番
❹ to move backwards	b a c k u p	375
❹ to hold someone or something tightly	h o l d o n t o	394
❹ to say that you do not agree with something	o b j e c t t o	376
❺ to eat something	f e e d o n	366
❺ to be accepted as something	p a s s f o r	401
❺ to be or look good together	g o t o g e t h e r	395
❺ to sell all of the available items, tickets, etc. and have none remaining	s e l l o u t	370
❺ to feel sympathy for someone	f e e l f o r	372
❺ to give support or help to someone or something	b a c k u p	375
❺ to say your opinion to oppose something publicly	s p e a k o u t a g a i n s t	369
❺ to make something possible	a l l o w f o r	368
❺ to be responsible for something	a n s w e r f o r	399
❺ to release someone or something	l e t o u t	392
❻ to get angry with someone	b l o w u p	405
❻ to avoid leaving a certain place	k e e p t o	365
❻ to try to avoid something bad happening	l o o k o u t f o r	398
❻ to consider something carefully	t h i n k o u t	387
❻ to test someone or something to see if they are suitable for something	t r y o u t	388
❻ to promise that someone has a certain quality or can be relied on	a n s w e r f o r	399
❻ to make something that will be sold to others	b r i n g o u t	364
❻ to give someone or something to someone else, especially because they have asked for it or should have it	h a n d o v e r	389
❻ to make a copy of something stored on a computer	b a c k u p	375
❻ to ask questions in order to find out more about something	i n q u i r e i n t o	391

語義	解答	連番
⑦ to say strongly and often that something is true, even if others do not think so	i n s i s t o n	379
⑦ to criticize someone or something unkindly	r u n d o w n	384
⑦ to end a relationship	b r e a k o f f	406
⑦ to stop something, such as a story or a conversation, especially before it is finished	l e a v e o f f	367
⑦ to cause someone to become sad, lose confidence, etc.	b r i n g d o w n	377
⑦ to be completely sold	s e l l o u t	370
⑦ to let yourself be controlled or influenced by something	s u r r e n d e r t o	386
⑦ to learn something in an informal way	p i c k u p	403
⑦ to stop following old beliefs and do something in a new or different way	b r e a k w i t h	402
⑦ to start doing something	g o a b o u t	371
⑧ to demand something and not be persuaded to accept anything else	i n s i s t o n	379

HOLD BACK (→446)

holdは「〜を(一時的に)つかんでいる、保つ」という意味の動詞、backは「後ろに」という意味の副詞で、組み合わせると「〜を引き留める」というイメージを表します。自分を引き留めると「ためらう；自制する」

という意味になり、人の前進や発展を引き留めると「〜を遅らせる、妨げる」という意味になります。

① ためらう；自制する

Don't **hold back**. Hit the punching bag as hard as you can.

(ためらうな。サンドバッグを思いっきり殴るんだ。)

② 〜を引き留める、食い止める

The woman was trying to attack the man, but her friends **held** her **back**.

(女性はその男に襲いかかろうとしたが、友人たちが引き留めた。)

③ 〈人の前進・発展など〉を遅らせる、妨げる

Some business leaders claim that the new regulations are going to **hold back** innovation.

(新しい規制はイノベーションを抑制することになると主張するビジネスリーダーもいる。)

④ 〈感情など〉を抑える

Apparently trying to **hold back** a sneeze is very dangerous.

(くしゃみを我慢するのはとても危険らしい。)

Stage 8

Rome wasn't built in a day.
ローマは一日にして成らず。

tear up
《tear 事物 up / tear up 事物》

〜を引き裂く

① to destroy something by ripping it into pieces

ずたずたに引き裂くことによって何かを破壊する

≒ rip up

例 Victoria **tore up** her homework in a fit of rage.

ヴィクトリアはかっとなって宿題をびりびりに破いた。

〈契約など〉を破棄する

② to refuse to accept something like an agreement

合意のようなものを受け入れることを拒否する

例 Threats to **tear up** the peace agreement have not been taken as seriously as they should be.

和平協定を破棄するという脅しは、本来あるべきほどには真剣に受け止められてこなかった。

fill in
《fill 事物 in / fill in 事物》

〈書類など〉に必要事項を記入する

to complete a document by giving all the needed information

必要な情報をすべて提供して文書を完成させる

≒ fill out

例 Once you **fill in** all your contact information, we can proceed with the rest of the appointment.

ご連絡先情報をすべてご記入いただくと、予約の続きを進めることができます。

《fill 人 in / fill in 人》

〈人〉に新しい情報を（詳細に）与える

to give someone information about something

何かについて誰かに情報を与える

例 Fred **filled in** his coworker on what had happened at the meeting.

フレッドは、会議で起きたことを同僚に詳しく伝えた。

□□□ 410

talk into *doing*
《talk 人 into *doing*》

| to convince someone to do something | 〈人〉を説得して〜させる |

誰かに何かをするよう説得する

⇔ talk out of doing

例 He couldn't believe that he'd let his wife **talk** him **into** watching a horror film.

彼は、妻に説得されてホラー映画を見ることになるとは思いもしなかった。

□□□ 411

come down with
《come down with 事物》

〈病気〉にかかる

412句

| to get an illness | 病気になる |

例 Burt **came down with** the flu twice last winter.

バートは去年の冬、インフルエンザに2回かかった。

□□□ 412

lay off
《lay 人 off / lay off 人》

（不況などで）〈人〉を一時解雇する

to stop employing someone because there is no work

仕事がないため誰かを雇うのをやめる

例 The company had to **lay off** hundreds of workers during the recession.

不況の間、その会社は何百人もの従業員を解雇しなければならなかった。

《lay off 事物》

〜を一時的にやめる

to stop using or doing something

何かを使ったり、したりするのをやめる

例 She had to **lay off** running for months after spraining her ankle.

足首を捻挫した後、彼女はランニングを何か月も休まなければならなかった。

□□□ **413**

count on
《count on 人》

to trust someone to do something

〈人〉を信頼する、頼る

誰かが何かをすることを信頼する

例 We're **counting on** you to bring the files on time.

私たちは、あなたが時間どおりにファイルを持ってきてくれるものと思っています。

《count on 事物》

to expect something to happen

～が起こることを期待する

何かが起こることを期待する

例 I was **counting on** a big bonus at the end of the year, but I didn't get one.

年末に多額のボーナスを期待していたが、もらえなかった。

□□□ **414**

keep out
《keep 人・事物 out / keep out 人・事物》

to stop someone or something from entering somewhere

～を中に入れない；
～を防ぐ

誰かまたは何かがどこかに入るのを止める

例 A huge fence **keeps** people **out** of the property.

巨大なフェンスがあって、敷地内には人が入れないようになっている。

□□□ **415**

part with
《part with 事物》

to give up owning or controlling something

〈大切なものなど〉を手放す

何かを所有したり管理したりすることをあきらめる

例 She didn't want to **part with** any of the puppies, but she just didn't have the space to keep all of them.

彼女はどの子犬も手放したくなかったが、すべての子犬を飼うスペースはなかった。

□□□ 416

put in
《put 事物 in / put in 事物》

〈設備など〉を備えつける

① to make something ready to be used in a specific place

何かを特定の場所で使える
ようにする

≒ install

例 They had a specialist **put in** their new dishwasher.

彼らは専門家に新しい食器洗
い機を設置してもらった。

〈一定の時間・労力〉を
費やす、注ぐ

417句

② to spend time and energy doing something

何かをして時間とエネル
ギーを費やす

例 Sara **put in** a lot of time and effort writing her thesis.

サラは論文の執筆に多くの時
間と労力を費やした。

《put in 事物》

〈言葉〉をはさむ、
つけ加える

to interrupt someone so that you can say something

自分が何かを言えるように
誰かの言葉を遮る

例 Could I **put in** a word before you continue?

話を続けられる前に、一言言っ
てもいいでしょうか。

□□□ 417

avail yourself of
《avail yourself of 事物》

～を利用する

to make use of something

何かを利用する

例 Please do not hesitate to **avail yourself of** every
amenity offered by the hotel.

当ホテルがご提供するあらゆ
るアメニティは遠慮なくご利用
ください。

keep back

《keep 事物 back / keep back 事物》

〈涙・笑いなど〉をこらえる

① to not show your emotions even when you want to show them

感情を表に出したくても表に出さない

例 He struggled to **keep back** his tears, especially in front of his family.

特に家族の前では、彼は涙をこらえるのに必死だった。

〈情報など〉を（一部）隠しておく

② to refuse to tell someone something

誰かに何かを言うのを拒否する

例 She **kept back** a lot of the details, not wanting to frighten anyone.

誰も怖がらせたくなかったので、彼女は詳細の多くを隠しておいた。

〜の一部を取っておく

③ to not use a part of something, such as an amount of money

何かの一部、例えば金額などの一部を使わない

例 Carson **kept back** half of his allowance every month.

カーソンは毎月、小遣いの半分を取っておいた。

pride yourself on

《pride yourself on 事物》

〜を誇りにする、
〜が自慢だ

to be proud of something

何かを誇りに思う

例 Carrie **prides herself on** how beautifully she can draw.

キャリーは、絵を美しく描けることを誇りに思っている。

□□□ 420

turn away
《turn 人 away / turn away 人》

〈人〉の入場を断る

to deny someone entry to a place

ある場所への誰かの立ち入りを拒否する

例 They got **turned away** at the door because they hadn't bought their tickets in advance.

彼らは前もってチケットを買っていなかったので、入り口で入場を断られた。

□□□ 421

break up
《break 事物 up / break up 事物》

～をばらばらにする

421句

① to separate something into smaller pieces

何かをより小さな断片に分ける

ⓘ 「ばらばらになる」という自動詞の使い方もある。

例 She **broke up** the carrots into smaller pieces.

彼女はにんじんを細かく刻んだ。

〈集会など〉を解散させる

② to make something end, such as a meeting or protest

集会や抗議など、何かを終わらせる

ⓘ 「〈集会などが〉解散する、終わる」という自動詞の使い方もある。

例 The police **broke up** the protest happening in front of city hall.

警察は、市役所の前で行われていた抗議行動を解散させた。

《break up》

（関係・愛情などが）終わる、（恋人などと）別れる

to end a relationship with someone

誰かとの関係を終わらせる

例 Allison **broke up** with her partner six months ago.

アリソンは半年前にパートナーと別れた。

□□□ **422**

draw out
《draw 事物 out / draw out 事物》

〈預金〉を引き出す

① to take money out of a bank account

銀行口座から金を引き出す

≒ withdraw

⇔ deposit

例 Sheldon **drew out** $100 from his bank account.

シェルドンは銀行口座から100ドル引き出した。

〈会議など〉を引き延ばす、長引かせる

② to make something last longer than usual

何かを通常より長く続かせる

≒ prolong

例 The interviewer tried to **draw out** the interview as long as he could.

インタビュアーは、できるだけ長くインタビューを引き延ばそうとした。

□□□ **423**

set down
《set 事物 down / set down 事物》

〈組織などが〉〈規定・指針など〉を決定する

① to state how something should be done

何かをどのように行うべきか述べる

例 The rules of the game have been **set down** clearly by the teacher.

ゲームのルールは先生によって明確に定められている。

～を書き留める、記録する

② to record something by writing it

書くことによって何かを記録する

例 Her therapist recommended that she **set down** her feelings in a journal.

セラピストは、自分の感じていることを日記に書き留めるよう彼女に薦めた。

□□□ 424

come before
《come before 人・事物》

〈問題などが〉〈検討・審議
のため〉〜に提出される

**to be presented to someone in authority,
such as a judge in a court, so that a decision
can be made**

決定を下すことができるよう
に、裁判所の裁判官のような
権限ある人に提示される

例 Your case will **come before** the courts in a few
months.

あなたの事件は数か月後に裁
判所に提出されるでしょう。

425句

□□□ 425

break down
《break down》

故障する

① **to stop working properly**

正常に動作しなくなる

ⓘ breakdown（故障）という語も覚えておこう。

例 Beck's car **broke down** in the middle of nowhere.

ベックの車は人里離れたところ
で故障した。

〈話し合い・計画などが〉
失敗する

② **to fail or stop being successful**

失敗する、または成功しなく
なる

≒ fall apart

例 The couple's marriage **broke down** quickly once they
moved in together.

そのカップルの結婚は、一緒に
住み始めるとすぐに破綻した。

取り乱す、泣き崩れる

③ **to lose control of yourself because of
strong emotions, especially sadness**

強い感情、特に悲しみのた
めに自分自身をコントロー
ルできなくなる

例 Benji **broke down** and started to cry while giving his
speech at the funeral.

ベンジーは葬儀でスピーチを
していて泣き崩れてしまった。

□□□ 426

make for
《make for 事物》

① to move toward a place

～の方へ（急いで）行く、向かう

ある場所に向かって移動する

≒ head for

例 Please remain calm and **make for** the nearest emergency exit.

落ち着いて、一番近い非常口に向かってください。

～に役立つ、寄与する

② to cause or help something to happen

何かを起こす、または何かが起きるのを助ける

例 Neither team was playing well, which **made for** a boring game to watch.

どちらのチームもいいプレイをしていなかったので、見ていてつまらない試合になった。

□□□ 427

knock down
《knock 人 down / knock down 人》

to make someone fall

〈人〉を倒す

誰かを倒す

≒ take down

例 Deanna ran past a group of kids and **knocked** one of them **down**.

ディアナは子どもたちの一団の間を駆け抜け、そのうちの1人を倒してしまった。

《knock 事物 down / knock down 事物》

〈建物・家具など〉を解体する

to destroy a building or part of one

建物またはその一部を破壊する

≒ demolish

例 The old movie theater got **knocked down** and is going to be replaced by a shopping mall.

その古い映画館は取り壊され、代わりにショッピングモールが建てられようとしている。

□□□ 428

put down
《put 事物 down / put down 事物》

〜を書き留める

① to write something

何かを書く

≒ write down

例 **Put down** your name and phone number here, and I'll call you as soon as I can.

こちらにお名前と電話番号を書いていただければ、できるだけ早くお電話します。

〈暴動・反乱など〉を鎮圧する

② to stop something dangerous by force

何か危険なものを力ずくで止める

≒ crush

例 The uprising was **put down** by military forces.

その反乱は、軍隊に鎮圧された。

《put 人 down / put down 人》

〈人〉を（人前で）こきおろす

to criticize someone and make them feel bad

誰かを批判して、その人を嫌な気分にさせる

例 You shouldn't **put** people **down** just because they didn't do something well on the first try.

1回目の挑戦でうまくいかなかったからといって、人をこきおろすべきではない。

□□□ 429

drive out
《drive 人・事物 out / drive out 人・事物》

〜を追い出す、追い払う

to make someone or something leave

誰かまたは何かを去らせる

例 Indigenous people throughout the world have been **driven out** of their ancestral lands.

世界中の先住民が、先祖代々の土地から追い出されてきた。

□□□ **430**

rest on

《rest on 人・事物》

〜にかかっている

---

① to depend on someone or something

誰かまたは何か次第である

例 Success in this industry **rests on** your ability to work hard.

この業界での成功は、一生懸命働く能力にかかっている。

〈視線が〉〜に注がれる

② to stop moving and look at someone or something

動くのをやめて、誰かまたは何かを見る

例 David's eyes **rested on** the sign for a few moments before he finally looked away.

デイビッドの目はしばらくその看板に注がれていたが、彼はやがて目をそらした。

《rest on 事物》

〜に基づく

to be based on something

何かに基づいている

例 The case against my client **rests** entirely **on** a few misguided assumptions.

私のクライアントに対する訴訟は、完全に、いくつかの誤った仮定に基づいている。

□□□ **431**

come through

《come through 事物》

〈病気・危機など〉を切り抜ける

to experience living through something

何かを切り抜けることを経験する

≒ survive

例 Peter was able to **come through** the operation without any major complications.

ピーターは大きな合併症もなく、手術を乗り切ることができた。

□□□ 432

ascribe to
《ascribe 事物 to 人・事物》

~を…のせいにする

to consider that something is caused by a specific thing or person

何かが特定のものや人によって引き起こされていると考える

例 This report **ascribes** the rise in animal extinctions **to** climate change.

この報告書は、動物の絶滅の増加を気候変動に起因するものとしている。

433句

《ascribe 事物 to 人》

〈作品・成果など〉を～のものと考える

to consider or say that something was written, made, etc. by a specific person

何かが特定の人によって書かれた、作られたなどと考えたり、言ったりする

例 That quote is **ascribed to** a famous philosopher, but it isn't known if he really said that.

その引用句は有名な哲学者のものとされているが、彼が本当にそう言ったかどうかはわからない。

□□□ 433

keep up
《keep 事物 up / keep up 事物》

〈物事〉をやり続ける、頑張り続ける

① to continue doing something or keep something from getting worse

何かをし続ける、または悪化させないようにする

例 Her boss told her to **keep up** the good work.

上司は彼女にその調子で頑張るようにと言った。

~を維持する、高いままにしておく

② to prevent something from losing quality

何かが質を落とすのを防ぐ

例 The activists **kept up** the pressure on the government to pass more clean energy bills.

活動家たちは、より多くのクリーンエネルギー法案を可決するよう、政府に圧力をかけ続けた。

set up

《set 事物 up / set up 事物》

〜を立てる、建てる

① to place or build something somewhere

何かをどこかに設置したり建てたりする

例 The police **set up** roadblocks to prepare for the parade later that afternoon.

その日の午後に行われるパレードに備え、警察はバリケードを設置した。

〈機械など〉を組み立てる、セットアップする

② to make a machine ready for use

機械を使えるようにする

例 It took hours to **set up** the new office printer.

オフィスの新しいプリンターをセットアップするのに何時間もかかった。

〈組織・制度など〉を設立する

③ to start an organization, committee, etc.

組織、委員会などを立ち上げる

≒ establish

例 Gerald **set up** his own export business when he was young.

ジェラルドは若い頃、自分の輸出会社を立ち上げた。

《set 人 up / set up 人》

〈人〉を陥れる、はめる

to cause someone to appear guilty or to be in a bad situation

誰かを有罪のように思わせたり、悪い状況に陥らせたりする

例 The woman claims that she was **set up** by her former spouse.

その女性は、元の配偶者にはめられたのだと主張している。

□□□ 435

take up

《take 事物 up / take up 事物》

〈話題・問題など〉を取り上げる

① to do something about a problem, suggestion, etc.

問題、提案などについて何かをする

例 The local newspaper has **taken up** a story about the protests.

地元の新聞は、抗議行動に関する話題を取り上げた。

435句

〜に興味を持つようになる；（趣味として）〜を始める

② to start to study or practice something new, especially as a hobby

特に趣味として、何か新しいことを勉強したり練習したりし始める

例 Elizabeth has **taken up** studying Chinese lately.

エリザベスは最近、中国語の勉強を始めた。

〈研究・仕事など〉を始める、〜に従事する

③ to start a new job or have a new responsibility

新しい仕事を始める、または新しい責任を負う

例 Penelope will **take up** the management of the marketing team starting next week.

ペネロペは来週からマーケティングチームのマネジメントを担当する。

《take up 事物》

〈時間・場所〉を占める、使う

to fill or use some space or time

空間または時間を埋める、または使う

例 The door-to-door salesperson promised not to **take up** too much of her time.

訪問販売員は、それほど彼女の時間はとらせないと約束した。

□□□ **436**

fit in
《fit in》

to be accepted by other people

例 Just be yourself, and don't worry too much about **fitting in** with the other kids.

適合する、
うまくやっていく

ほかの人々によって受け入
れられる

自分らしくしてなさい。ほかの
子たちに溶け込もうと心配しす
ぎなくていいんだよ。

□□□ **437**

reduce to
《reduce 人・事物 to 事物》

to make someone or something be in a worse condition than it was before

例 The giant earthquake **reduced** the town **to** rubble.

〜を〈好ましくない状態
など〉に変える

誰かまたは何かを以前より
も悪い状態にする

その巨大地震で、町はがれきと
化した。

□□□ **438**

see through
《see through 人・事物》

to realize what someone or something is really like

例 She was able to **see through** his façade and see who he really was.

〈隠れた本質〉を見抜く、
〈人〉の本質を見破る

誰かまたは何かが本当はど
のようなものであるかに気
づく

彼女は彼のうわべを見破り、本
当はどんな人かを理解すること
ができた。

□□□ **439**

dispense with
《dispense with 事物》

to stop using something

≒ do away with

例 Let's **dispense with** the formalities and get down to business.

〜を省く、廃止する

何かを使うのをやめる

形式的なことは抜きにして、本
題に入りましょう。

□□□ 440

set off

《set off》

（旅行などに）出発する

to start a journey

旅を始める

例 His family **set off** on a trip to the countryside.

彼の家族は、地方へ旅行に出かけた。

440句

《set 事物 off / set off 事物》

〈出来事など〉を引き起こす、始めさせる

① to make something start or happen

何かを開始させる、または生じさせる

例 Her actions **set off** events that would change her for the rest of her life.

彼女の行動は、残りの人生を変えてしまうほどの出来事を引き起こした。

〈爆弾など〉を爆発させる

② to make something explode

何かを爆発させる

例 The explosives were **set off** after everyone was a safe distance away.

爆発物は皆が安全な距離まで離れてから爆破された。

〈警報装置など〉を作動させる

③ to make an alarm start ringing

アラームを鳴り始めさせる

例 The thief **set off** the alarm when she entered the store.

泥棒が店に侵入すると、警報機が鳴った。

□□□ **441**

go through with
《go through with 事物》

to do something that you have talked about or thought about doing

〈計画・約束など〉を遂行する

しようと話していたこと、または思っていたことをする

例 Hannah decided at the last minute that she couldn't **go through with** dying her hair purple.

ハンナは土壇場になって、髪を紫に染めることはできないと思った。

□□□ **442**

ask after
《ask after 人・事物》

to ask how someone or something is doing

〈人の安否・健康〉を尋ねる

誰かまたは何かがどうなっているか尋ねる

ⓘ イギリス英語。

例 When Calvin saw Jack and Jill at the store, he **asked after** their son.

店でジャックとジルに会ったとき、カルヴィンは彼らの息子が元気かと尋ねた。

□□□ **443**

identify with
《identify 事物 with 事物》

to think that something is the same as something else

〜を…と同一視する

何かをほかの何かと同じであると考える

例 He argued that it is a mistake to **identify** being rich **with** being successful.

彼は金持ちであることと成功することを同一視するのは間違いだと主張した。

《identify 人 with 事物》

to think that someone is very closely related to or involved with something

〈人〉を〜と結びつけて考える

誰かが何かに非常に密接に関係している、または関与していると考える

例 Eric has long been **identified with** radical groups.

エリックは長い間、過激派と関係があると考えられてきた。

□□□ 444

settle down
《settle down》

〈気持ちなどが〉落ち着く

① to become quiet and calm

静かで落ち着いた状態になる

ⓘ 「〈人〉を落ち着かせる」という他動詞の使い方もある。

例 Once everyone **settles down**, I'll start the lecture.

みんなが静かになったら講義を始めます。

445句

身を落ち着ける

② to get into a comfortable position

快適な姿勢になる

例 Damon **settled down** on the sofa to watch his favorite TV show.

デイモンはソファにゆったり腰を下ろして、お気に入りのテレビ番組を見た。

身を固める

③ to start to live a quiet and steady life

静かで安定した生活を始める

例 It has always been Vicky's dream to **settle down** in the suburbs and raise a family.

郊外に落ち着いて家庭を築くのが、ずっとヴィッキーの夢だった。

□□□ 445

hand out
《hand 事物 out / hand out 事物》

〜を配る、配布する

to give something to other people

ほかの人たちに何かを与える

≒ distribute

例 There was a young man **handing out** flyers in front of the bus stop.

バス停の前でチラシを配っている若い男性がいた。

hold back
《**hold back**》

ためらう；自制する

---

to stop yourself from doing something

自分が何かをするのをやめる

例 During the meeting, Tessa **held back** and didn't mention her own opinion.

会議の間、テッサは我慢して自分の意見を言わなかった。

《hold 人・事物 back / hold back 人・事物》

〜を引き留める、食い止める

---

① to make someone or something stop moving forward

誰かまたは何かが前進するのを止める

例 Logan **held back** the man to keep him from running into the fire.

ローガンは、男性が火の中に走っていかないよう引き留めた。

〈人の前進・発展など〉を遅らせる、妨げる

② to stop the progress of someone or something

誰かまたは何かの進行を止める

例 Many economists feel that the economy is being **held back** by government policies.

多くの経済学者が、政府の政策によって経済が抑制されていると感じている。

《hold 事物 back / hold back 事物》

〈感情など〉を抑える

to not allow yourself to feel or show a particular emotion

特定の感情を感じたり、表に出したりすることを自分に許さない

例 Bonnie **held back** tears as her daughter walked down the aisle.

娘が教会の通路を歩いていく間、ボニーは涙をこらえていた。

□□□ 447

work out
《work out》

運動をする、体を鍛える

① to exercise in order to improve your health or physical fitness

健康または体力を向上させるために運動する

447句

ⓘ workout（運動、トレーニング）という語も覚えておこう。

例 Emily **works out** at the gym four times per week.

エミリーは週に4回、ジムで運動をしている。

〈物事が〉（結局は）うまくいく

② to develop or happen successfully

発展する、または成功する

例 Everything will surely **work out** as long as you do your best.

ベストを尽くせば、きっとすべてうまくいきますよ。

《work 事物 out / work out 事物》

〈問題など〉を解決する、解く

to find the answer to something

何かの答えを見つける

例 Claire managed to **work out** all of the math problems on her assignment.

クレアは、宿題の数学の問題を何とかすべて解くことができた。

《work 人・事物 out / work out 人・事物》

〈物事〉をなんとか理解する；〈人〉の性格がわかる

to understand how someone or something is

誰かまたは何かがどのようであるかを理解する

ⓘ イギリス英語。

例 The plot of the movie was so complicated that he couldn't **work** it **out**.

その映画の筋はとても複雑で、彼には理解できなかった。

章末ボキャブラリーチェック

次の語義が表す英熟語を答えてください。

語義	解答	連番
❶ to write something	p u t d o w n	428
❷ to make something last longer than usual	d r a w o u t	422
❸ to state how something should be done	s e t d o w n	423
❹ to fill or use some space or time	t a k e u p	435
❺ to exercise in order to improve your health or physical fitness	w o r k o u t	447
❻ to not use a part of something, such as an amount of money	k e e p b a c k	418
❼ to prevent something from losing quality	k e e p u p	433
❽ to be presented to someone in authority, such as a judge in a court, so that a decision can be made	c o m e b e f o r e	424
❾ to stop something dangerous by force	p u t d o w n	428
❿ to refuse to accept something like an agreement	t e a r u p	408
⓫ to lose control of yourself because of strong emotions, especially sadness	b r e a k d o w n	425
⓬ to place or build something somewhere	s e t u p	434
⓭ to make something explode	s e t o f f	440
⓮ to continue doing something or keep something from getting worse	k e e p u p	433
⓯ to realize what someone or something is really like	s e e t h r o u g h	438
⓰ to be accepted by other people	f i t i n	436
⓱ to stop moving and look at someone or something	r e s t o n	430
⓲ to cause someone to appear guilty or to be in a bad situation	s e t u p	434
⓳ to criticize someone and make them feel bad	p u t d o w n	428
⓴ to start an organization, committee, etc.	s e t u p	434
㉑ to refuse to tell someone something	k e e p b a c k	418
㉒ to experience living through something	c o m e t h r o u g h	431

語義	解答	連番
㉓ to give up owning or controlling something	p a r t w i t h	415
㉔ to expect something to happen	c o u n t o n	413
㉕ to do something about a problem, suggestion, etc.	t a k e u p	435
㉖ to interrupt someone so that you can say something	p u t i n	416
㉗ to consider or say that something was written, made, etc. by a specific person	a s c r i b e t o	432
㉘ to depend on someone or something	r e s t o n	430
㉙ to make someone fall	k n o c k d o w n	427
㉚ to understand how someone or something is	w o r k o u t	447
㉛ to think that something is the same as something else	i d e n t i f y w i t h	443
㉜ to make an alarm start ringing	s e t o f f	440
㉝ to cause or help something to happen	m a k e f o r	426
㉞ to find the answer to something	w o r k o u t	447
㉟ to record something by writing it	s e t d o w n	423
㊱ to make a machine ready for use	s e t u p	434
㊲ to complete a document by giving all the needed information	f i l l i n	409
㊳ to get into a comfortable position	s e t t l e d o w n	444
㊴ to start to study or practice something new, especially as a hobby	t a k e u p	435
㊵ to be based on something	r e s t o n	430
㊶ to give someone information about something	f i l l i n	409
㊷ to stop yourself from doing something	h o l d b a c k	446
㊸ to start to live a quiet and steady life	s e t t l e d o w n	444
㊹ to convince someone to do something	t a l k i n t o *d o i n g*	410
㊺ to stop using or doing something	l a y o f f	412
㊻ to make something start or happen	s e t o f f	440
㊼ to make use of something	a v a i l y o u r s e l f o f	417

❹ to spend time and energy doing something — put in — 416

❹ to start a journey — set off — 440

❺ to make something ready to be used in a specific place — put in — 416

❺ to trust someone to do something — count on — 413

❺ to make someone or something be in a worse condition than it was before — reduce to — 437

❺ to take money out of a bank account — draw out — 422

❺ to fail or stop being successful — break down — 425

❺ to separate something into smaller pieces — break up — 421

❺ to not allow yourself to feel or show a particular emotion — hold back — 446

❺ to make someone or something leave — drive out — 429

❺ to destroy something by ripping it into pieces — tear up — 408

❺ to think that someone is very closely related to or involved with something — identify with — 443

❻ to stop someone or something from entering somewhere — keep out — 414

❻ to develop or happen successfully — work out — 447

❻ to stop working properly — break down — 425

❻ to make someone or something stop moving forward — hold back — 446

❻ to do something that you have talked about or thought about doing — go through with — 441

❻ to move toward a place — make for — 426

❻ to end a relationship with someone — break up — 421

❻ to stop using something — dispense with — 439

❻ to consider that something is caused by a specific thing or person — ascribe to — 432

❻ to destroy a building or part of one — knock down — 427

❼ to ask how someone or something is doing — ask after — 442

語義	解答	連番
❼ to make something end, such as a meeting or protest	<u>break up</u>	421
❼ to not show your emotions even when you want to show them	<u>keep back</u>	418
❼ to stop employing someone because there is no work	<u>lay off</u>	412
❼ to get an illness	<u>come down with</u>	411
❼ to stop the progress of someone or something	<u>hold back</u>	446
❼ to become quiet and calm	<u>settle down</u>	444
❼ to be proud of something	<u>pride yourself on</u>	419
❼ to start a new job or have a new responsibility	<u>take up</u>	435
❼ to deny someone entry to a place	<u>turn away</u>	420
❽ to give something to other people	<u>hand out</u>	445

COME AROUND (→455)

comeは「来る」という意味の動詞、aroundは「周りを回って」という意味の副詞で、組み合わせると「ぐるっと回って（戻って）来る」イメージの句動詞になります。行事などであれば「（周期的に）巡ってくる」という意味になり、人が来る場合は、ここを目指して直線的にやって来るというよりも、ほかの場所にも寄りながら「ぶらりとやって来る」イメージ。さらに、意見などについて使うと、紆余曲折を経ながらも最終的に「（相手の意見などに）同調することにする」という意味を表します。

① 〈行事などが〉（周期的に）巡ってくる

A total solar eclipse like this only **comes around** once every hundred years.

（このような皆既日食は100年に一度しか起こらない。）

② （人を）（ぶらりと）訪問する

You should **come around** to my office sometime. We'll get lunch.

（今度、私のオフィスに寄ってください。お昼を食べましょう。）

③ （相手の意見などに）同調することにする

He eventually **came around** to the idea of being a stay-at-home dad.

（彼は最終的に、専業主夫になるという考えを受け入れるに至った。）

Stage 9

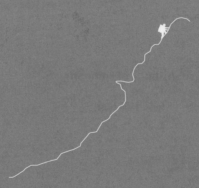

Put your best foot forward.
ベストを尽くせ。

□□□ 448

engage in
《engage in 事物》

〜に従事する、
参加する

to take part in something

何かに参加する

例 She just hoped that her son wasn't **engaging in** any criminal activities.

彼女はただ、息子が犯罪行為に手を染めていないことを祈るだけだった。

《engage 人 in 事物》

〈人〉を〜に従事させる、参加させる

to make someone take part in something

誰かを何かに参加させる

例 Georgia tried really hard to **engage** the guests **in** conversation.

ジョージアは懸命に、客たちを会話に参加させようとした。

□□□ 449

fall on
《fall on 事物》

〈日付などが〉〜にあたる

① to happen on a specific day or date

特定の日または日付に起こる

例 The lunar eclipse just happened to **fall on** my birthday.

その月食は偶然、ちょうど私の誕生日と重なった。

〈責任などが〉〜に降りかかる

② to be the responsibility of someone

誰かの責任である

例 The party expenses all **fell on** the host.

そのパーティーの費用は、すべて主催者の負担になった。

□□□ 450

come by
《come by》

立ち寄る

to visit someone

誰かを訪ねる

例 Why don't you **come by** after work tomorrow?

明日、仕事の後に寄っていかない?

451句

《come by 事物》

〜を（苦労して）手に入れる

to manage to get something

なんとかして何かを手に入れる

≒ obtain

例 This fruit is hard to **come by** in winter.

この果物は冬にはなかなか手に入らない。

□□□ 451

throw up
《throw up》

（食べ物を）吐く、戻す

to have something from your stomach come out through your mouth

胃の中のものを口から出す

≒ vomit

ⓘ 「〜を吐く」という他動詞の使い方もある。

例 She had such a bad stomachache that it caused her to **throw up**.

彼女は腹痛がひどくて吐いてしまった。

《throw 事物 up / throw up 事物》

〈ほこりなど〉を巻き上げる；〈建物〉を大急ぎで建てる

to raise, lift, or build something quickly

何かを素早く上げる、持ち上げる、または建てる

例 I feel like they **threw up** that house across the street overnight.

彼らは通りの向かいの家を一晩で建ててしまったかのようだ。

□□□ **452**

lay out
《lay 事物 out / lay out 事物》

~を広げる、並べる

① to spread something out

何かを広げる

例 Ursula **laid out** all her receipts on the table so she could organize them.

アーサラは、整理できるように領収書をすべてテーブルの上に広げた。

~を設計する

② to arrange something in a specific way

何かを特定の仕方で配置する

例 The town was **laid out** specifically to be easy to walk around.

その町は、歩き回りやすいように特別に設計された。

~を詳しく説明する

③ to explain the details of something

何かの詳細を説明する

≒ set out

例 The instructions for building this cabinet are **laid out** very clearly.

このキャビネットの組み立て説明書は、とてもわかりやすく説明されている。

□□□ **453**

put off
《put 事物 off / put off 事物》

~を延期する、遅らせる

to decide to do something at a later time

何かを後ですることにする

≒ postpone, delay

例 Katherine **put off** writing her report until the very last minute.

キャサリンは、報告書を書くのをぎりぎりまで先延ばしにした。

□□□ 454

get across
《get 事物 across / get across 事物》

〈話〉をわからせる、
理解させる

to communicate something clearly so that it can be understood

理解されるように何かを明確に伝える

455句

ⓘ「〈話が〉伝わる、理解してもらえる」という自動詞の使い方もある。

例 It took a while, but she finally **got** her point **across**.

少し時間はかかったが、彼女は最終的に自分の言いたいことを理解してもらえた。

□□□ 455

come around
《come around》

〈行事などが〉（周期的に）巡ってくる

① to happen again

再び起こる

例 The carnival **comes around** every summer at this time.

毎年、夏のこの時期にカーニバルが開催される。

（人を）（ぶらりと）訪問する

② to visit someone at their house

誰かをその家に訪問する

例 You should **come around** for a visit soon.

近いうちに訪ねてきてください。

（相手の意見などに）
同調することにする

③ to stop opposing or disagreeing with someone or something

誰かまたは何かに反対したり異議を唱えたりするのをやめる

例 He'll eventually **come around** to the idea.

彼は、最終的にはその考えに同調するだろう。

□□□ **456**

single out
《single 人·事物 out / single out 人·事物》

~だけを選ぶ、取り上げる

to choose someone or something out of a group to receive special attention

特別に注目されるように、誰かまたは何かをグループから選ぶ

例 The coach **singled** her **out** for missing the previous practice.

コーチは前回の練習をさぼったということで彼女を名指しした。

□□□ **457**

turn to
《turn to 人·事物》

~に頼る

to go to someone or something for help

誰かまたは何かに助けを求めに行く

例 Remember that you can always **turn to** your mother for help when you need it.

助けが必要なときには、いつでもお母さんに頼れることを忘れないでね。

□□□ **458**

tell on
《tell on 人》

〈人〉のことを言いつける、告げ口する

to tell someone in power about the bad behavior of someone else

権力のある人に、ほかの人の悪い行動について話す

例 Christina always **told on** bullies when she was in school.

クリスティーナは学校に通っていた頃、いつもいじめっ子のことを言いつけていた。

《tell on 人·事物》

~にこたえる、悪影響を与える

to have a noticeable effect on someone or something

誰かまたは何かに顕著な影響を与える

例 The lack of sleep is really beginning to **tell on** him.

睡眠不足は彼にかなり悪影響を与え始めている。

□□□ 459

come down to
《come down to 事物》

〜に行きつく、帰結する

to depend on one important point

一つの重要な点次第である

例 It all **comes down to** if you want doves at your wedding or not.

結局のところ、すべてはあなたが結婚式にハトを使いたいかどうかだ。

460句

《come down to 人》

〈伝統・風習などが〉〈人〉に伝わる、受け継がれる

to be passed between people over a long period of time

長期間にわたって人々の間で受け渡される

例 The stories that have **come down to** us from our ancestors are incomplete.

先祖から私たちに受け継がれてきたその物語は不完全だ。

□□□ 460

come off
《come off》

〈ボタン・柄などが〉取れる、外れる

① to become separated from something

何かから分離する

(i) 〈come off 事物〉（〜から取れる、外れる）という使い方もある。

例 Her nail polish has gradually **come off**.

彼女のマニキュアは次第に剥がれてきた。

〈計画などが〉成功する、実現する

② to be successful

成功する

例 Their first performance at the music hall **came off** very well.

音楽ホールでの彼らの初演奏は大成功だった。

☐☐☐ 461

fix up
《fix 事物 up / fix up 事物》

~を修理する、
手入れする

to repair or improve something

何かを修理したり改善した
りする

≒ do up

例 Jayden decided that he would **fix up** the old car for his father.

ジェイデンは、父親のために古
い車を修理することにした。

《fix 人 up / fix up 人》

〈人〉に用意 [手配] する

to give someone something that they want

誰かにその人が欲しがって
いる何かを与える

例 Do you think you could **fix** me **up** with a room for the night?

今夜、私に部屋を手配してもら
うことはできそうですか。

☐☐☐ 462

inquire after
《inquire after 人》

〈人〉の安否 [様子] を尋
ねる

to ask for information about someone, especially about their health or what they are doing

誰かについて、特にその人
の健康や何をしているかに
ついての情報を求める

例 Foster was **inquiring after** you at the meeting last night.

フォスターが昨夜の会合で、あ
なたが元気かどうか尋ねてい
ましたよ。

☐☐☐ 463

hang around with
《hang around with 人》

〈人〉と何となく時間を
過ごす

to spend a lot of time with someone

誰かと多くの時間を過ごす

ⓘ hang around も参照。

例 His mother was worried about the people he was **hanging around with**.

彼の母親は、彼がつるんでいる
人たちのことで心配していた。

□□□ 464

put forth
《put forth 事物》

〈考えなど〉を述べる、提案する

① to suggest something for people to think about

人々に何かについて考えるように提案する

≒ submit

例 The ideas that you **put forth** in that last meeting were excellent.

前回の会議であなたが提案したアイデアは素晴らしかったです。

〈芽・葉など〉を出す

② to develop new leaves, shoots, etc.

新しい葉や芽などを成長させる

例 The apple tree in the front yard has started to **put forth** new leaves.

前庭のリンゴの木が新しい葉を出し始めた。

□□□ 465

stand out
《stand out》

目立つ、人目につく

① to be easily seen or noticed

簡単に見える、または気づかれる

例 Her blue hair really **stands out** in a crowd.

彼女の青い髪は人混みの中でとても目立つ。

際立つ、抜きんでている

② to be more important than someone or something

誰かや何かよりも重要である

ⓘ outstanding（際立った）という語も覚えておこう。

例 That summer **stands out** to me as the best in my life.

あの夏は、私にとって人生で最高の夏として際立っている。

465句

□□□ 466

throw out
《throw 事物 out / throw out 事物》

～を投げ出す、捨てる

to get rid of something

何かを処分する

例 Ralph **threw out** all of his textbooks when he graduated.

ラルフは卒業すると教科書をすべて処分した。

《throw 人 out / throw out 人》

〈人〉を追放する

to make someone leave a place, especially because they have done something wrong

特に何か悪いことをしたという理由で、誰かをある場所から去らせる

例 The two men were **thrown out** of the club for causing a fight.

2人の男性は、けんかを起こしてクラブから追放された。

□□□ 467

trust with
《trust 人 with 事物》

〈人〉に～を委ねる、預ける

to let someone have or use something of value

誰かに価値あるものを持たせたり、使わせたりする

例 You can **trust** her **with** your dogs, as she is very responsible.

彼女はとても責任感が強いので、安心して犬を預けることができますよ。

□□□ 468

pass out
《pass out》

気絶する、意識を失う

to fall asleep or become unconscious

眠りに落ちる、または意識がなくなる

≒ faint

⇔ come to

例 Emma **passed out** from the pain of breaking her leg.

エマは脚の骨折の痛みで意識を失った。

□□□ 469

face up to
《face up to 事物》

〈嫌なことなど〉を受け入れる、〜に対処する

to accept or deal with something that is hard or unpleasant

難しかったり不快だったりする何かを受け入れたり、それに対処したりする

471句

例 Since you are the one who did it, you have to **face up to** the consequences.

あなたがやったのだから、その結果にもあなたが対処しなければなりません。

□□□ 470

get down to
《get down to 事物》

〈仕事など〉に（本腰を入れて）取りかかる

to start to give your attention to something difficult

何か難しいことに注意を向け始める

例 We need to **get down to** work if we're going to finish this plan in time for the meeting.

もしこの計画を会議に間に合うように完成させるつもりなら、私たちは仕事に取りかかる必要がある。

□□□ 471

rule out
《rule 事物 out / rule out 事物》

〜（の可能性など）を除外する

① to decide that something is impossible or not suitable

何かが不可能または適切でないと判断する

例 We **ruled out** allowing alcohol at the party so that everyone could attend.

私たちは、誰でも参加できるように、パーティーでの飲酒は認めないことにした。

〜を不可能にする、できなくする

② to make something impossible

何かを不可能にする

例 The climate here **rules out** a lot of farming options.

ここの気候では、多くの農作物は育たない。

227

□□□ **472**

dwell on
《dwell on 事物》

〜についてよくよく考える、くどくど述べる

to think or talk about something for too long

何かについてあまりに長時間、考えたり話したりする

例 **Dwelling on** the past will just upset you.

過去のことをくよくよ考えても、心が乱れるだけです。

□□□ **473**

cross out
《cross 事物 out / cross out 事物》

〜を（線を引いて）消す

to draw a line through a word

ある言葉の上に線を引く

例 The teacher got all the students to **cross out** any incorrect answers on their worksheets.

先生は生徒全員に、課題シートの不正解を線で消させた。

□□□ **474**

catch on
《catch on》

〈もの・考えが〉流行する

① to become popular

人気が出る

例 It took a while for high-rise jeans to **catch on** again.

ハイライズジーンズが再び流行するまでには、しばらく時間がかかった。

わかる、感づく

② to learn or understand something

何かを知る、または理解する

例 It wasn't until they saw him in action that the police **caught on** to what he was trying to do.

彼の動きを見てようやく、警察は彼がしようとしていることに感づいた。

□□□ **475**

lay down
《lay 事物 down / lay down 事物》

〈武器など〉を捨てる

① to put something down and stop using it, especially a weapon

何か、特に武器を置き、使うのをやめる

476句

例 **Lay down** your weapon and put your hands on your head!

武器を捨てて、手を頭の上に置け!

〈規則・法など〉を決める、規定する

② to tell other people what to do or how to feel in a strong or rude way

ほかの人々に強く、または無礼な仕方で、何をすべきか、どう感じるかを伝える

例 Rufus **laid down** the rules without asking anyone their opinion.

ルーファスは、誰の意見も聞かずにルールを決めた。

□□□ **476**

let down
《let 人 down / let down 人》

〈人〉を失望させる、〈人〉の期待を裏切る

to make someone unhappy by not being as good as expected

期待されたほどよくないことで誰かを不幸にする

例 Roxy **let down** her father when she didn't get into a top college.

ロキシーは一流大学に入ることができず、父親を失望させた。

《let 事物 down / let down 事物》

～を降ろす、下げる

to make or let something move down

何かを下に移動させる、またはそれを可能にする

例 The construction worker slowly **let down** the lumber to his coworker.

建設作業員は、材木を同僚のところまでゆっくりと降ろした。

□□□ 477

hold out
《hold out》

〈供給などが〉持つ

---

① to last or continue to exist

持続する、または存在し続ける

例 Water supplies won't **hold out** if we don't get some rain soon.

すぐに雨が降らないと、水の供給が持たない。

（攻撃などに）持ちこたえる

---

② to continue to resist

抵抗し続ける

例 The rebels were able to **hold out** for weeks in the jungle.

反乱軍はジャングルの中で何週間も持ちこたえることができた。

《hold 事物 out / hold out 事物》

〈手など〉を差し出す

---

to reach out your hand or arm toward someone

誰かに向かって手や腕を伸ばす

例 The little girl **held out** her hand to the puppy, and he licked it.

少女が子犬に手を差し出すと、子犬はその手をなめた。

□□□ 478

go along with
《go along with 人・事物》

〈人・計画・決定など〉に賛成する

---

to agree with someone or something

誰かまたは何かに同意する

例 They decided to just **go along with** what he was saying because it was easier than arguing.

言い争うより楽なので、彼らは彼が言っていることにただ賛成することにした。

□□□ 479

put forward
《put 事物 forward / put forward 事物》

〈意見・案など〉を出す、
提案する

① to suggest something to discuss

議論用に何かを提案する

480句

≒ propose

例 The team **put forward** a number of suggestions to the CEO.

チームはCEOにいくつかの提案をした。

〜の日程を繰り上げる

② to move something to an earlier time

何かをより早い時間に移動させる

≒ move forward, move up

例 The final match of the day has been **put forward** to 3 P.M.

その日の最終試合は午後3時に繰り上げられた。

□□□ 480

cut in
《cut in》

（会話などに）口をはさむ

① to interrupt and join a conversation suddenly

突然会話を遮り、そこに参加する

例 Sorry to **cut in** on you, but could you repeat what you just said?

遮ってすみませんが、今言われたことをもう一度言っていただけますか。

〈車・運転者が〉（列などに）割り込む

② to suddenly drive in front of another vehicle in a dangerous way

突然、危険な仕方でほかの車の前に車を移動させる

例 Don't **cut in** like that. You'll cause an accident.

そんなふうに割り込まないで。事故を起こしちゃうよ。

take off

《take off》

〈飛行機などが〉離陸する

---

① to start flying

飛び始める

⇔ land

ⓘ takeoff（離陸）という語も覚えておこう。

例 The plane **took off** from the airport on time.

飛行機は定刻に空港を離陸した。

（急に）立ち去る

② to go somewhere in a hurry

急いでどこかに行く

例 Mario **took off** in a hurry after receiving a call.

マリオは電話を受けると、急いで立ち去った。

急にうまくいくようになる

③ to suddenly start being successful

突然成功し始める

例 Her career really started to **take off** after she released that album.

彼女のキャリアは、そのアルバムを出した後急にうまく回り出した。

《take 事物 off / take off 事物》

〈服・靴など〉を脱ぐ

to remove a piece of clothing

衣服を脱ぐ

⇔ put on

例 The room was really hot, so he **took off** his sweater.

その部屋はとても暑かったので、彼はセーターを脱いだ。

□□□ 482

take in

《take 事物 in / take in 事物》

〈空気など〉を吸い込む；
〈食物・水など〉を摂取する

① to allow something to enter your body

482句

何かが体に入ることを許す

ⓘ intake（吸入、摂取）という語も覚えておこう。

例 Wanda **took in** a lot of water when she fell off the boat.

ワンダはボートから落ちたときに大量の水を飲んだ。

〈映画・名所など〉を見に行く

② to go see or visit something

何かを見に行く、または訪れる

例 They always **take in** a film when they go to the city.

彼らは街に行くときはいつも映画を見に行く。

〈意味・状況など〉を理解する

③ to understand or remember something that you have learned

学んだことを理解したり覚えたりする

例 She didn't **take** anything **in** from the seminar last night.

彼女は、昨夜のセミナーで何も得るものがなかった。

《take 人 in / take in 人》

〈人〉をだます、かつぐ

to make someone believe something that is not true

誰かに真実ではないことを信じさせる

≒ deceive

例 You shouldn't be **taken in** by his charm.

彼の魅力にだまされてはいけません。

take out

《take 事物 out / take out 事物》

～を取り出す、持ち出す

---

① to move something from a place

ある場所から何かを移動する

例 Jennifer **took** the rice **out** of the cupboard to cook it.

ジェニファーは、米を炊くために戸棚から米を取り出した。

〈異物・虫歯など〉を摘出する、抜く

② to remove something from a person, place, or thing

人、場所、ものから何かを取り除く

例 When did you have your wisdom teeth **taken out**?

あなたはいつ親知らずを抜いてもらったんですか。

〈食べ物〉をテイクアウトする

③ to buy cooked food to take somewhere else to eat

ほかの場所に持っていって食べるために、調理済みの食べ物を買う

ⓘ takeout（持ち帰り用の料理）という語も覚えておこう。

例 Will this order be to dine in or to **take out**?

この注文は、店内で召し上がるのでしょうか、それともお持ち帰りでしょうか。

《take 人 out / take out 人》

〈人〉を（レストラン・映画などに）連れていく

to go somewhere with someone you have invited

招待した人とどこかに行く

例 Her mother **took** her **out** for dinner to celebrate her promotion.

彼女の母親は、昇進を祝うために彼女を食事に連れていった。

clear up

《clear up》

〈空が〉晴れ上がる

① to change so that there are no clouds or fog

雲や霧がないように変わる

例 We won't be able to climb the mountain if the weather doesn't **clear up** soon.

すぐに天気がよくならないと、私たちは山に登れないだろう。

〈病気などが〉よくなる

② (of an illness, infection, etc.) to go away

（病気・感染症などが）なくなる

例 Luckily it only took a few days for his cold to **clear up**.

幸い、彼の風邪が治るまで数日しかかからなかった。

《clear 事物 up / clear up 事物》

～を片づける

① to make a place clean or tidy

場所をきれいにする、または整頓する

例 Let's **clear up** all of the trash before your friends arrive.

友だちが到着する前に、ごみを全部片づけましょう。

〈問題など〉を解決する、説明する

② to solve or explain something

何かを解決する、または説明する

例 We need to **clear up** a few points before we can move on.

次に進む前に、私たちはいくつかの点を解決しておく必要がある。

□□□ **485**

take to
《take to 人・事物》

～が好きになる

to start to like someone or something

誰かまたは何かを好きにな
り始める

例 Their dog **took to** the new kittens right away.

彼らの犬は、新しい子猫たちが
すぐに好きになった。

《take to *doing*》

～が習慣になる、
～するようになる

to start to do something as a habit

習慣として何かをし始める

例 Dee has **taken to** jogging before work.

ディーは、仕事の前にジョギン
グをするようになった。

《take to 事物》

（休息・逃亡などのため
に）～に向かう

to go to a place

場所に行く

例 The rebels **took to** the mountains to escape.

反乱軍は逃げるために山に向
かった。

□□□ **486**

push forward
《push forward》

（困難に負けず）突き進む

to continue moving or traveling to a place, even when it is far or difficult to get to

遠く、または行きにくい場合
でも、ある場所に移動また
は旅行を続ける

例 Since there is only a few kilometers left, let's just **push forward** for a little longer.

あと数キロしか残っていない
から、もう少しだけ進み続けま
しょう。

□□□ 487

hold up
《hold up》

(よい状態で)続く、
持ちこたえる

487句

to continue to be strong and effective

強力かつ効果的であり続ける

例 This truck is **holding up** really well, considering that it's almost twenty years old.

このトラックは、20年近く前のものであることを考えると、とてもよく持ちこたえている。

《hold 人・事物 up / hold up 人・事物》

〈手など〉を上げる；
～を持ち上げる

① to keep someone or something from falling

誰かまたは何かが落ちないように保つ

例 Mackenzie **held up** his sister so she could see the beautiful view safely.

マッケンジーは、美しい景色を安全に見られるように妹を持ち上げた。

～(の進行)を遅らせる、
邪魔する

② to delay someone or something

誰かまたは何かを遅らせる

例 The meeting was **held up** due to technical difficulties.

技術的な問題で会議が遅れた。

《hold up 事物》

(武装して)～を襲って
金品を奪う

to steal something from a place using violence

暴力を使ってある場所から何かを盗む

例 Three masked individuals **held up** a security van in the neighborhood last night.

昨夜、近所で覆面をした3人組が現金輸送車を襲ってお金を奪った。

章末ボキャブラリーチェック

次の語義が表す英熟語を答えてください。

語義	解答	連番
❶ to make someone unhappy by not being as good as expected	let down	476
❷ to be successful	come off	460
❸ to put something down and stop using it, especially a weapon	lay down	475
❹ to decide to do something at a later time	put off	453
❺ to arrange something in a specific way	lay out	452
❻ to make someone take part in something	engage in	448
❼ to steal something from a place using violence	hold up	487
❽ to get rid of something	throw out	466
❾ to suggest something for people to think about	put forth	464
❿ to ask for information about someone, especially about their health or what they are doing	inquire after	462
⓫ to learn or understand something	catch on	474
⓬ to move something to an earlier time	put forward	479
⓭ to start to do something as a habit	take to	485
⓮ to continue moving or traveling to a place, even when it is far or difficult to get to	push forward	486
⓯ to last or continue to exist	hold out	477
⓰ to let someone have or use something of value	trust with	467
⓱ to choose someone or something out of a group to receive special attention	single out	456
⓲ to make something impossible	rule out	471
⓳ to make someone leave a place, especially because they have done something wrong	throw out	466
⓴ to make or let something move down	let down	476
㉑ to spend a lot of time with someone	hang around with	463

語義	解答	連番
㉒ to go see or visit something	take in	482
㉓ to develop new leaves, shoots, etc.	put forth	464
㉔ to solve or explain something	clear up	484
㉕ to have something from your stomach come out through your mouth	throw up	451
㉖ to remove a piece of clothing	take off	481
㉗ to fall asleep or become unconscious	pass out	468
㉘ to agree with someone or something	go along with	478
㉙ to become separated from something	come off	460
㉚ to raise, lift, or build something quickly	throw up	451
㉛ to repair or improve something	fix up	461
㉜ to depend on one important point	come down to	459
㉝ to go somewhere in a hurry	take off	481
㉞ to delay someone or something	hold up	487
㉟ to start to give your attention to something difficult	get down to	470
㊱ to go somewhere with someone you have invited	take out	483
㊲ to go to someone or something for help	turn to	457
㊳ to happen again	come around	455
㊴ to suggest something to discuss	put forward	479
㊵ to have a noticeable effect on someone or something	tell on	458
㊶ to remove something from a person, place, or thing	take out	483
㊷ to think or talk about something for too long	dwell on	472
㊸ to make a place clean or tidy	clear up	484
㊹ to draw a line through a word	cross out	473
㊺ to allow something to enter your body	take in	482
㊻ to tell other people what to do or how to feel in a strong or rude way	lay down	475
㊼ to continue to resist	hold out	477

❹ to suddenly start being successful — take off — 481

❹ to be more important than someone or something — stand out — 465

❺ to stop opposing or disagreeing with someone or something — come around — 455

❺ to be the responsibilty of someone — fall on — 449

❺ to be easily seen or noticed — stand out — 465

❺ to move something from a place — take out — 483

❺ to interrupt and join a conversation suddenly — cut in — 480

❺ to buy cooked food to take somewhere else to eat — take out — 483

❺ to explain the details of something — lay out — 452

❺ to visit someone — come by — 450

❺ to communicate something clearly so that it can be understood — get across — 454

❺ to take part in something — engage in — 448

❻ (of an illness, infection, etc.) to go away — clear up — 484

❻ to keep someone or something from falling — hold up — 487

❻ to make someone believe something that is not true — take in — 482

❻ to be passed between people over a long period of time — come down to — 459

❻ to become popular — catch on — 474

❻ to start flying — take off — 481

❻ to decide that something is impossible or not suitable — rule out — 471

❻ to visit someone at their house — come around — 455

❻ to understand or remember something that you have learned — take in — 482

❻ to go to a place — take to — 485

❼ to tell someone in power about the bad behavior of someone else — tell on — 458

語義	解答	連番
❼ to suddenly drive in front of another vehicle in a dangerous way	c u t i n	480
❼ to spread something out	l a y o u t	452
❼ to manage to get something	c o m e b y	450
❼ to accept or deal with something that is hard or unpleasant	f a c e u p t o	469
❼ to start to like someone or something	t a k e t o	485
❼ to give someone something that they want	f i x u p	461
❼ to change so that there are no clouds or fog	c l e a r u p	484
❼ to happen on a specific day or date	f a l l o n	449
❼ to reach out your hand or arm toward someone	h o l d o u t	477
❽ to continue to be strong and effective	h o l d u p	487

TAKE ON (→504)

takeは「〜を(手に)取る」という意味の動詞、onは接触を意味する副詞で、組み合わせると「何かを手に取って自分のところに引き受ける」イメージの句動詞となります。ビジネスの場面で人をtake onす

るのは「〈人〉を雇う、採用する」という意味。また戦闘や試合、論戦などで人をtake onするのは、「〈人〉を対戦相手として引き受ける」→「〈人〉と戦う」という意味。さらに仕事や責任を「引き受ける」という意味や、性質や様相を「引き受ける」→「帯びる」という意味も表します。

①〈人〉を雇う、採用する

The company will have to stop **taking on** new employees for a while.

(その会社はしばらくの間、新入社員の採用を中止せざるを得ない。)

②〈人〉と戦う

If Japan beats Brazil in this game, they'll **take on** Germany next week.

(日本がこの試合でブラジルに勝てば、来週はドイツと対戦することになる。)

③〈仕事など〉を引き受ける；〈責任など〉を負う

Even though my schedule is full, I keep **taking on** new work commitments.

(スケジュールはいっぱいだが、次々と新しい仕事を引き受けている。)

④〈性質・様相など〉を帯びる、呈する

His wife's face **took on** an embarrassed look when he was incorrectly explaining how stocks work.

(彼が株の仕組みを間違って説明したとき、彼の妻は恥ずかしそうな表情を浮かべた。)

Stage 10

The best view comes after the hardest climb.
最高の景色は最も辛い登りの先にひらける。

□□□ **488**

talk back to
《talk back to 人》

〈人〉に口答えする

to answer someone in a rude way

失礼な仕方で誰かに答える

例 She taught all of her children that it was rude to **talk back to** teachers.

彼女は子どもたち全員に、教師に口答えするのは失礼だと教えた。

□□□ **489**

bring on
《bring 事物 on / bring on 事物》

〈病気・災害など〉を引き起こす

to make something bad happen

何か悪いことを起こす

≒ cause

例 Running in the cold **brought on** an asthma attack.

寒い中を走ったことで喘息の発作が出た。

□□□ **490**

relate to
《relate to 人・事物》

～に関連している

① to be connected with someone or something

誰かまたは何かと関係がある

例 All emails **relating to** the next big marketing campaign should be sent to the section chief as well.

今度の大規模なマーケティングキャンペーンに関するメールはすべて、セクションチーフにも送るようにしてください。

～に共感する

② to be able to understand and feel sympathy for someone or something

誰かまたは何かを理解したり、共感したりできる

≒ empathize with

例 We can all **relate to** what you're going through right now.

私たちは皆、あなたが今経験していることについて、お気持ちが理解できます。

□□□ 491

go for
《go for 人・事物》

491句

① to go somewhere to get someone or something

〈もの〉を取り[買い]に
行く；〈人〉を呼びに行く

誰かまたは何かを得るため
にどこかに行く

例 Mom has just **gone for** some coffee.

お母さんならコーヒーを買い
に行ってる。

〜を好む、
〜が気に入る

② to like someone or something

誰かまたは何かが好きである

例 She **goes for** tall men with facial hair.

彼女は、ひげを生やした背の
高い男性が好みだ。

《go for 人》

〜を攻撃する

to attack someone

誰かを攻撃する

例 The woman **went for** him with a stick.

その女性は、杖で彼を攻撃した。

《go for 事物》

〜を選ぶ、
〜のほうを取る

to choose something

何かを選ぶ

例 Let's **go for** the all-you-can-eat pizza plan.

ピザ食べ放題のプランにしよう。

grow out of
《grow out of 事物》

〜から生じる、起こる

① to develop from something

何かから発展する

例 That law **grew out of** a need to protect children from dangerous lawn toys.

その法律は、危険な芝生のおもちゃから子どもたちを守る必要性から生まれた。

（体が成長して）〈服など〉が合わなくなる

② to become too large for a certain piece of clothing

特定の衣服に対して大きくなりすぎる

≒ outgrow

例 Caroline cried when she **grew out of** her favorite dress.

キャロラインは、お気に入りのワンピースが入らなくなって泣いた。

（成長して）〜を脱する

③ to stop doing a certain thing as you get older

年を取るにつれて特定のことをしなくなる

≒ outgrow

例 The doctor told her that her son would **grow out of** sucking his thumb eventually.

医師は彼女に、息子さんは大きくなればいずれ親指をしゃぶらなくなりますよと言った。

report to
《report to 人》

〈人〉の直属の部下である

to be managed by someone at work and have to give information to them regularly

職場で誰かに管理され、その人に定期的に情報を伝えなければならない

例 The Vice President of Sales **reports** directly **to** the CEO.

営業担当副社長は、CEOの直属の部下だ。

□□□ 494

wind up
《**wind up**》

(〜という)はめ［結果］
になる

to be in a place or situation that was not expected, especially an unpleasant one

予想していなかった、特に
不快な場所や状況にいる

≒ end up

例 Dallas wasn't quite sure how he'd **wound up** on a rollercoaster.

ダラスは、どうしてジェットコー
スターに乗るはめになったの
か、よくわからなかった。

《**wind** 事物 **up** / **wind up** 事物》

〜を終える、結ぶ

to bring something to an end

何かを終わらせる

例 Now that all the presentations are over, it's time to **wind** things **up**.

これですべてのプレゼンが終
わりましたので、そろそろ終わ
りにしましょう。

□□□ 495

come away
《**come away**》

〈柄・ボタンなどが〉取れ
る、外れる

① **to become separated from something**

何かから分離する

例 The wallpaper has started to **come away** from the wall in a few places.

壁紙がところどころ剥がれ始め
ている。

(〜から)離れる、去る

② **to move away from a place with a specific feeling or idea**

特定の感情や考えを持って
ある場所から離れる

例 We **came away** with the impression that he was an honest and ethical salesperson.

私たちは、彼が誠実で倫理的
な販売員であるという印象を
持って、その場を後にした。

□□□ 496

give back
《give 人 事物 back / give 人 back 事物》

〜を〈人〉に返す、戻す

① to return something to its owner

何かを持ち主に返す

ⓘ 人 は〈to＋人〉の形で後ろに置くこともある。

例 Olive made sure to **give** her teacher the pencil **back** at the end of class.

オリーブは、授業の終わりに忘れずに先生に鉛筆を返した。

〈人〉に〜を再び与える、再び享受させる

② to make it possible for someone to have something again

誰かが再び何かを持つことを可能にする

≒ restore

例 Yalcin had a large operation to **give** him **back** his sight.

ヤルシンは視力を回復するために大きな手術を受けた。

□□□ 497

catch at
《catch at 事物》

〈もの〉をつかもうとする

to try to hold something

何かをつかもうとする

例 He **caught at** her arm as she started to walk away.

彼女が立ち去りかけると、彼は彼女の腕をつかもうとした。

□□□ 498

put through
《put 人・事物 through》

〈電話・人〉を（相手に）つなぐ

to connect someone to someone else by phone

電話で誰かとほかの誰かをつなぐ

例 Please wait a few minutes, and we will **put** you **through** to the sales department.

少々お待ちください。販売部におつなぎします。

☐☐☐ **499**

interfere with
《interfere with 事物》

~を妨げる、
~の邪魔をする

500句

to prevent something from succeeding or happening as planned

何かが成功したり計画どおりに起こったりするのを妨げる

例 Poor mental health is known to **interfere with** performance in all aspects of life.

心の不調は、生活のあらゆる面でパフォーマンスを妨げることが知られている。

☐☐☐ **500**

drop off
《drop off》

うとうとと眠ってしまう

① to fall asleep

眠りに落ちる

≒ nod off

例 Tim **dropped off** while he was watching a movie.

ティムは映画を見ている間にうとうと眠ってしまった。 .

〈数量などが〉減少する

② to become fewer or less

数や量が少なくなる

例 The number of participants has been **dropping off** steadily for the past few years.

ここ数年で参加者数は着実に減っている。

《drop 人・事物 off / drop off 人・事物》

~を届ける、置いてくる

to take someone or something somewhere and then leave

誰かをどこかに連れていき、または何かを持っていき、そして去る

例 Your father will **drop** you **off** at school tomorrow instead of me.

明日は私の代わりにお父さんがあなたを学校まで送っていきます。

□□□ 501

be derived from
《be derived from 事物》

~に由来する

to develop or come from another thing

別のものから発展したり、生まれたりする

ⓘ derive from もほぼ同じ意味。

例 This medication **is derived from** a rare plant located in the jungle.

この薬は、ジャングルにある希少な植物に由来する。

□□□ 502

make off
《make off》

急いで逃げる

to leave quickly to escape

逃げるために急いで立ち去る

例 The thieves **made off** just as the police arrived.

警察が到着するとすぐに泥棒は急いで逃げた。

□□□ 503

bump into
《bump into 人・事物》

（誤って）~にぶつかる

to hit someone or something by mistake

間違って誰かまたは何かにぶつかる

例 Harry accidentally **bumped into** the girl when he walked past her.

ハリーは少女とすれ違うとき、うっかり彼女にぶつかってしまった。

《bump into 人》

〈人〉に偶然出くわす

to meet someone you know by chance

偶然に知っている誰かに会う

≒ run into

例 Susan **bumped into** her old friend at the farmer's market.

スーザンはファーマーズ・マーケットで旧友に偶然会った。

□□□ 504

take on
《take 人 on / take on 人》

〈人〉を雇う、採用する

504句

① to employ someone

誰かを雇う

例 Our company will be **taking on** 45 new employees next month.

当社は来月、45人の新入社員を採用する。

〈人〉と戦う

② to play or fight against someone in a game or contest

ゲームやコンテストで誰かと対戦したり戦ったりする

例 France will **take on** Japan in the first of several soccer games next Sunday.

フランスは来週の日曜日、サッカーの複数の試合のうちの初戦で日本と戦う。

《take 事物 on / take on 事物》

〈仕事など〉を引き受ける；〈責任など〉を負う

① to start to deal with something

何かを扱い始める

例 Don't **take on** more work if it will negatively affect your health.

健康に悪影響を及ぼすようなら、これ以上仕事を引き受けるのはやめなさい。

〈性質・様相など〉を帯びる、呈する

② to start to have a specific quality or appearance

特定の質または外観を持ち始める

例 Her face **took on** a solemn look when she saw the mess.

彼女はそのめちゃくちゃな状態を見て、険しい表情を浮かべた。

□□□ **505**

fall into
《fall into 事物》

〜に分類される

① to belong to a specific category

特定のカテゴリーに属する

例 Readers of this book series will **fall into** one of two categories.

この本のシリーズの読者は、2つのカテゴリーのどちらかに入る。

〜に陥いる

② to suddenly be a certain way

突然、ある状態になる

例 The local museum has **fallen into** disrepair in recent years.

地元の博物館は近年、急激に荒廃してきている。

□□□ **506**

cover up
《cover up》

身を包む、服を着る

to cover yourself or part of yourself with something

自分自身または自分の一部を何かで覆う

ⓘ cover yourself up とも言う。

例 Connor likes to keep **covered up** in the summer so he doesn't get a sunburn.

コナーは日焼けをしないように、夏も肌を出さないようにしている。

《cover 事物 up / cover up 事物》

〈事実・失敗など〉を隠ぺいする

to keep people from learning the truth about something

人々が何かについての真実を知ることができないようにする

例 The council was accused of **covering up** several scandals involving the mayor.

議会は、市長にまつわる複数の疑惑を隠蔽していると非難された。

□□□ 507

get away with
《get away with 事物》

① to steal something and escape with it

例 The thieves **got away with** all the jewels.

〜を持ち逃げする

509句

何かを盗み、それを持って
逃げる

泥棒は宝石を全部持って逃げた。

**② to do something bad and not be
punished or criticized for it**

例 Every year, many people cheat when taking that exam
and **get away with** it.

〜のとがめを受けない

何か悪いことをしても、その
ことで罰せられたり批判さ
れたりしない

毎年、その試験で多くの人がカン
ニングをし、つかまらずにいる。

□□□ 508

brush up
《brush 事物 up / brush up 事物》

**to improve or practice a skill that you have
not used for a long time**

① brush up on という形も使われる。

例 Keisha decided to **brush up** her Korean before her trip
to Seoul.

〜に磨きをかける

長い間使っていないスキル
を向上させたり、練習したり
する

ケイシャは、ソウル旅行の前に
韓国語に磨きをかけておくこと
にした。

□□□ 509

burn up
《burn 事物 up / burn up 事物》

to destroy something using fire

① 「燃え尽きる」という自動詞の使い方もある。

例 Harold **burned up** all of his diaries so no one else
could ever read them.

〜を燃やし尽くす

火を使って何かを破壊する

ハロルドは、誰も読むことがで
きないように、日記を全部燃や
した。

provide for
《provide for 事物》

〜に備える

① to make plans to deal with something that might happen in the future

将来起こるかもしれない何かに対処するための計画を立てる

例 The general failed to **provide for** the possibility of an air attack.

軍の司令官は空爆の可能性に備えていなかった。

〈法律などが〉〜を認める

② to make it possible for something to be done

何かができるようにする

例 The work contract **provides for** two weeks of paid holidays.

労働契約では、2週間の有給休暇が与えられる。

《provide for 人・事物》

〜を養う、〜に必要なものを与える

to supply what is needed for someone or something

誰かまたは何かに必要なものを与える

例 Barry has worked hard his whole adult life to **provide for** his children.

バリーは子どもたちを養うために、大人になってからずっと働きづめだ。

fall back on
《fall back on 人・事物》

〜を頼みの綱とする

to use someone or something for help when you are not in a good situation

自分がよい状況にないとき、誰かまたは何かを助けに使う

例 We can always **fall back on** our savings if the new business fails.

新しいビジネスが失敗しても、いつでも貯蓄に頼ることができる。

□□□ 512

draw on
《draw on》

to pass gradually

〈日時が〉(ゆっくりと)過ぎていく

513句

徐々に過ぎていく

例 As the trip **drew on**, everyone started to get a little bit grumpy.

旅行が進むにつれ、みんなは少し不機嫌になり始めた。

《draw on 事物》

to use knowledge or skills to do something

〈知識・経験など〉を利用する、あてにする

何かを作るために知識や技術を使う

例 She **drew on** her knowledge as a nurse to save the young man's life.

彼女は看護師としての知識を駆使して、その若い男性の命を救った。

□□□ 513

point to
《point to 事物》

① to mention something because you feel it is important

〜に言及する

重要だと思い、何かに言及する

例 Many people have **pointed to** the need for more financial support for students.

多くの人が、学生への経済的支援がもっと必要だと指摘している。

② to show that something is true or likely true

〜を示す、表す

何かが真実である、または真実である可能性が高いことを示す

例 All of the evidence we have collected **points to** her guilt.

私たちが集めた証拠はすべて、彼女が有罪であることを示している。

stand up for
《stand up for 人·事物》

〜を支持する、守る

---

to defend someone or something

誰かまたは何かを擁護する

例 Haley always **stands up for** her brother, regardless of the situation.

ヘイリーは、どんな状況でも常に弟の側に立つ。

tell off
《tell 人 off / tell off 人》

〈人〉を叱りつける

---

to speak angrily to someone because they did something wrong

間違ったことをしたという理由で、誰かに対して怒って話す

例 Felix **told off** his brother for playing his video games without asking permission.

フェリックスは、弟が無断で彼のテレビゲームをしたので叱りつけた。

draw up
《draw up》

〈車が〉止まる

---

to arrive and stop at a place

ある場所に到着して止まる

例 She got into the taxi that **drew up** to the gate.

彼女は、門のところで止まったタクシーに乗り込んだ。

《draw 事物 up / draw up 事物》

〈文書など〉を作成する

to make a written document in a proper or official way

適切なまたは公式な仕方で文書を作成する

例 Marcus finally **drew up** his will.

マーカスはついに遺言書を作成した。

□□□ 517

sit back
《sit back》

① to sit on something in a relaxed position

例 Niamh **sat back** on the sofa with a book in her hand.

ゆったり座る、くつろぐ

リラックスした姿勢で何か
に座る

ニアムは本を片手にソファでく
つろいだ。

手を出さない、
傍観する

② to make no effort to do something

例 Leon just **sat back** and watched everyone argue with
each other.

何かをしようと努力しない

レオンは傍観しているだけで、み
んなが言い合うのを見ていた。

□□□ 518

set forth
《set forth》

to begin a journey

≒ set out

例 The group **set forth** on a journey across Europe.

出発する

旅を始める

一行はヨーロッパ横断の旅に
出た。

《set 事物 forth / set forth 事物》

to present something

例 Mike **set forth** his plan to reduce homelessness in the
city at the council meeting.

～を表明 [説明] する

何かを提示する

マイクは、市内のホームレスを
減らすための計画を議会で説
明した。

□□□ 519

conjure up
《conjure 事物 up / conjure up 事物》

（魔法で）〜を出す

① to make something appear by using magic

魔法を使って何かを出現させる

例 My favorite character is the one who can **conjure up** storms.

私の大好きなキャラクターは嵐を起こすことができるキャラクターだ。

〈記憶・イメージなど〉を思い出させる

② to cause someone to imagine something

誰かに何かを想像させる

≒ evoke

例 Thinking of exercise always seems to **conjure up** images of marathon runners for me.

運動というと、私はいつもマラソンランナーをイメージしてしまうようなのです。

□□□ 520

trifle with
《trifle with 人・事物》

〜を軽く扱う、もてあそぶ

to treat someone or something without respect

敬意を払わずに誰かまたは何かを扱う

例 The CEO is not a woman to be **trifled with**.

そのCEOは、軽く扱われるような女性ではない。

□□□ 521

pass down
《pass 事物 down / pass down 事物》

（下の世代に）〜を伝える

to give something to a younger person, usually in your family

通常は家族の中で、より若い人に何かを渡す

≒ hand down

例 The vase has been **passed down** within our family for generations.

この花瓶は、我が家で代々受け継がれてきた。

□□□ 522

524句

give up on
《give up on 人・事物》

〜を見限る

to stop hoping that someone or something will change or get better at something

誰または何かが変わったり何かにおいてよくなったりすることを期待するのをやめる

例 It is really important that you don't **give up on** him.

あなたが彼を見限らないことが本当に重要です。

□□□ 523

send in
《send 事物 in / send in 事物》

〜を送付する、提出する

to mail or email something somewhere

何かをどこかに郵送またはメールで送る

例 You should **send in** your application before the end of the week if you want it to arrive in time.

もし間に合うように到着させたければ、今週末までに申請書を送ってください。

□□□ 524

add up to
《add up to 事物》

合計〜となる

① to have a number as a total

合計としてある数を持つ

例 Your order **adds up to** a total of $150.

ご注文は合計150ドルとなります。

結局〜ということになる

② to have a particular result

特定の結果を得る

例 The team's hard work planning for the event **added up to** a very successful fundraiser.

チームが苦労して立てたイベントの計画は、募金活動を大成功に導いた。

□□□ 525

wipe out
《wipe 人・事物 out / wipe out 人・事物》

〜を全滅させる、
壊滅させる

to kill or destroy someone or something completely

誰かまたは何かを完全に殺す、または破壊する

例 The tribe was completely **wiped out** by disease.

その部族は病気で完全に滅んだ。

《wipe 人 out / wipe out 人》

〈人〉をくたくたに疲れさせる

to make someone feel very tired

誰かに非常に疲れを感じさせる

例 Working that double shift has completely **wiped** me **out**.

二重シフトで働いて、私はくたくたに疲れ果てた。

□□□ 526

put across
《put 事物 across / put across 事物》

〜を（人に）わからせる

to make something be clearly understood

何かをはっきりと理解させる

例 Vanessa worked really hard to **put across** all of her points clearly and effectively.

ヴァネッサは言いたいことがすべて明確かつ効果的に伝わるようにとても努力した。

□□□ 527

jump at
《jump at 事物》

〈チャンスなど〉に飛びつく

to excitedly accept a chance to do something

何かをする機会をわくわくしながら受け入れる

例 Rodney **jumped at** the opportunity to go to Florida.

ロドニーはフロリダに行くチャンスに飛びついた。

□□□ 528

burn out
《burn out》

〈ろうそくなどが〉燃え尽きる

① to stop burning

燃えるのをやめる

ⓘ burn itself out とも言う。

例 The fire **burned out** in the early hours of the morning.

火は朝早い時間に燃え尽きた。

〈人が〉エネルギーを使い果たす

② to work so hard that you get sick and cannot continue working

一生懸命に働きすぎて病気になり、仕事を続けられなくなる

ⓘ burnout（燃え尽き症候群）という語も覚えておこう。

例 The overtime at her job caused her to **burn out**.

彼女は仕事で残業してエネルギーを使い果たした。

□□□ 529

let up
《let up》

〈風雨・痛みなどが〉やわらぐ、弱まる

① to become weaker

より弱くなる

例 The rain **let up** after a few hours.

雨は数時間後に弱まった。

力を抜く、気を緩める

② to stop working as hard as you were before

以前のように一生懸命働くのをやめる

例 He couldn't afford to **let up** if he wanted that promotion.

彼はその昇進を望むなら、手を抜くわけにはいかなかった。

☐☐☐ **530**

get by
《get by》

to have enough money for what you need, but not any extra

何とか生活していく

必要なだけの金はあるが、余分は一切ない

例 Grace earns just enough money to **get by**.

グレースは何とか暮らしていけるだけのお金を稼いでいる。

☐☐☐ **531**

dawn on
《dawn on 人》

to be realized or understood by someone for the first time

〈人〉にわかり始める

誰かによって初めて認識される、または理解される

例 It only **dawned on** her what his words meant long after he'd said them.

彼の言葉の意味が彼女にわかり始めたのは、彼が言ってずいぶん経ってからだった。

☐☐☐ **532**

embark on
《embark on 事物》

① to begin a journey

〈冒険など〉に乗り出す

旅を始める

例 They **embarked on** their journey together earlier today.

彼らは今日、一緒に旅に出た。

~を始める、
~に着手する

② to start something new or difficult

新しいことや難しいことを始める

例 Frankie **embarked on** a new career as an interpreter.

フランキーは、通訳としての新たなキャリアを始めた。

534句

□□□ 533

fall in with
《fall in with 人》

〈人〉と付き合うようになる

to meet a person or group by chance and become friendly with them

人やグループに偶然会い、親しくなる

≒ get in with

例 Stefanie **fell in with** the wrong crowd when she went to university.

ステファニーは大学に行って、悪い連中と付き合うようになった。

《fall in with 事物》

〜に同意する

to agree with someone's ideas or choices

誰かの考えや選択に同意する

例 Agatha **fell in with** his plans after hearing the details.

アガサは詳細を聞いて、彼の計画に同意した。

□□□ 534

pay off
《pay off》

〈努力・投資などが〉効果を生む

to produce a good result

よい結果を生み出す

例 Luckily his gamble **paid off**.

幸いなことに、彼の賭けは成功した。

《pay 事物 off / pay off 事物》

〈借金〉を完済する

to return all the money you owe someone

誰かに借りているすべての金を返す

例 Jackie finally **paid off** her student loans.

ジャッキーはついに学生ローンを完済した。

□□□ **535**

pass over
《pass 人 over / pass over 人》

〈人〉を（昇進などの候補から）外す

to not choose someone for a position

誰かをある地位に選ばない

例 Brian was **passed over** for the managerial position at his company.

ブライアンは、会社の管理職候補から外された。

□□□ **536**

fall through
《fall through》

失敗に終わる

to be incomplete or not happen

不完全である、または起こらない

例 Sadly her plans to go on a European tour **fell through**.

悲しいことに、ヨーロッパツアーに行く彼女の計画は実現しなかった。

□□□ **537**

back out
《back out》

手を引く

to not do something that you had agreed to do before

前にすることに同意していたことをしない

例 If you **back out** now, you will have to pay a cancellation fee.

今おやめになると、キャンセル料をお支払いいただかなければなりません。

□□□ **538**

cut back
《cut 事物 back / cut back 事物》

〜を削減する、縮小する

to reduce something

何かを減らす

ⓘ cut back onという形も使われる。cutback（削減、縮小）という語も覚えておこう。

例 Her doctor told her she had to **cut back** her calorie intake.

彼女は主治医から、カロリーの摂取を減らすように言われた。

□□□ 539

hold down
《hold 事物 down / hold down 事物》

~を抑える

① to keep something from rising

何かが上昇するのを抑える

例 The government has decided not to **hold down** prices despite severe inflation.

深刻なインフレにもかかわらず、政府は物価を抑制しないことを決定した。

〈仕事〉を続ける

② to continue to do a job for some time

ある仕事をしばらくの間続ける

例 Mr. King had to **hold down** a full-time job while also freelancing on the side.

キングさんはフルタイムの仕事を続けながら、副業としてフリーランスの仕事もしなければならなかった。

□□□ 540

back down
《back down》

引き下がる、撤回する

to admit you were wrong or that you have lost an argument

自分が間違っていたこと、または論争で負けたことを認める

例 Medford refused to **back down** despite the fact that he had no basis for his argument.

メドフォードは、自分の主張に根拠がないにもかかわらず、引き下がろうとしなかった。

□□□ 541

get in on
《get in on 事物》

〈活動など〉に加わる

to become involved in something that others are doing or planning

他人がやっている、または計画している何かに関与する

例 We would pay handsomely to be allowed to **get in on** this project.

このプロジェクトに参加させてもらえるなら、私たちは気前よく支払いましょう。

章末ボキャブラリーチェック

次の語義が表す英熟語を答えてください。

語義	解答	連番
❶ to defend someone or something	stand up for	514
❷ to agree with someone's ideas or choices	fall in with	533
❸ to return something to its owner	give back	496
❹ to move away from a place with a specific feeling or idea	come away	495
❺ to make a written document in a proper or official way	draw up	516
❻ to stop doing a certain thing as you get older	grow out of	492
❼ to meet a person or group by chance and become friendly with them	fall in with	533
❽ to stop burning	burn out	528
❾ to make it possible for someone to have something again	give back	496
❿ to mail or email something somewhere	send in	523
⓫ to speak angrily to someone because they did something wrong	tell off	515
⓬ to be managed by someone at work and have to give information to them regularly	report to	493
⓭ to stop working as hard as you were before	let up	529
⓮ to make someone feel very tired	wipe out	525
⓯ to continue to do a job for some time	hold down	539
⓰ to arrive and stop at a place	draw up	516
⓱ to play or fight against someone in a game or contest	take on	504
⓲ to be incomplete or not happen	fall through	536
⓳ to mention something because you feel it is important	point to	513
⓴ to suddenly be a certain way	fall into	505

語義	解答	連番
㉑ to keep people from learning the truth about something	c o v e r u p	506
㉒ to have a number as a total	a d d u p t o	524
㉓ to kill or destroy someone or something completely	w i p e o u t	525
㉔ to admit you were wrong or that you have lost an argument	b a c k d o w n	540
㉕ to like someone or something	g o f o r	491
㉖ to become weaker	l e t u p	529
㉗ to bring something to an end	w i n d u p	494
㉘ to steal something and escape with it	g e t a w a y w i t h	507
㉙ to be realized or understood by someone for the first time	d a w n o n	531
㉚ to keep something from rising	h o l d d o w n	539
㉛ to treat someone or something without respect	t r i f l e w i t h	520
㉜ to belong to a specific category	f a l l i n t o	505
㉝ to leave quickly to escape	m a k e o f f	502
㉞ to develop from something	g r o w o u t o f	492
㉟ to use knowledge or skills to do something	d r a w o n	512
㊱ to work so hard that you get sick and cannot continue working	b u r n o u t	528
㊲ to begin a journey	s e t f o r t h	518
㊳ to show that something is true or likely true	p o i n t t o	513
㊴ to make something be clearly understood	p u t a c r o s s	526
㊵ to improve or practice a skill that you have not used for a long time	b r u s h u p	508
㊶ to cause someone to imagine something	c o n j u r e u p	519
㊷ to do something bad and not be punished or criticized for it	g e t a w a y w i t h	507
㊸ to make something bad happen	b r i n g o n	489
㊹ to answer someone in a rude way	t a l k b a c k t o	488

❹❺ to connect someone to someone else by phone — put through — 498

❹❻ to start to have a specific quality or appearance — take on — 504

❹❼ to become involved in something that others are doing or planning — get in on — 541

❹❽ to supply what is needed for someone or something — provide for — 510

❹❾ to go somewhere to get someone or something — go for — 491

❺⓿ to start something new or difficult — embark on — 532

❺❶ to prevent something from succeeding or happening as planned — interfere with — 499

❺❷ to give something to a younger person, usually in your family — pass down — 521

❺❸ to stop hoping that someone or something will change or get better at something — give up on — 522

❺❹ to present something — set forth — 518

❺❺ to destroy something using fire — burn up — 509

❺❻ to take someone or something somewhere and then leave — drop off — 500

❺❼ to employ someone — take on — 504

❺❽ to become fewer or less — drop off — 500

❺❾ to return all the money you owe someone — pay off — 534

❻⓿ to be connected with someone or something — relate to — 490

❻❶ to pass gradually — draw on — 512

❻❷ to reduce something — cut back — 538

❻❸ to become separated from something — come away — 495

❻❹ to be in a place or situation that was not expected, especially an unpleasant one — wind up — 494

❻❺ to have a particular result — add up to — 524

❻❻ to make no effort to do something — sit back — 517

❻❼ to meet someone you know by chance — bump into — 503

❻❽ to have enough money for what you need, but not any extra — get by — 530

語義	解答	連番
❻ to not do something that you had agreed to do before	back out	537
❼ to excitedly accept a chance to do something	jump at	527
❼ to become too large for a certain piece of clothing	grow out of	492
❼ to produce a good result	pay off	534
❼ to choose something	go for	491
❼ to use someone or something for help when you are not in a good situation	fall back on	511
❼ to hit someone or something by mistake	bump into	503
❼ to cover yourself or part of yourself with something	cover up	506
❼ to sit on something in a relaxed position	sit back	517
❼ to try to hold something	catch at	497
❼ to attack someone	go for	491
❽ to not choose someone for a position	pass over	535
❽ to be able to understand and feel sympathy for someone or something	relate to	490
❽ to make it possible for something to be done	provide for	510
❽ to begin a journey	embark on	532
❽ to make something appear by using magic	conjure up	519
❽ to fall asleep	drop off	500
❽ to develop or come from another thing	be derived from	501
❽ to start to deal with something	take on	504
❽ to make plans to deal with something that might happen in the future	provide for	510

N

O

P

［編者紹介］

ロゴポート

語学書を中心に企画・制作を行っている編集者ネットワーク。編集者、翻訳者、ネイティブスピーカーなどから成る。おもな編著に『英語を英語で理解する 英英英単語® 初級編／中級編／上級編／超上級編』、『英語を英語で理解する 英英英単語® TOEIC® L&Rテスト スコア800／990』、『中学英語で読んでみる イラスト英英英単語®』、『最短合格! 英検®1級／準1級 英作文問題完全制覇』、『最短合格! 英検®2級 英作文&面接 完全制覇』、『出る順で最短合格! 英検®1級／準1級 語彙問題完全制覇 [改訂版]』、『出る順で最短合格!英検®準1級〜3級単熟語EX』(ジャパンタイムズ出版)、『TEAP単熟語Grip1500』(アスク出版)、『英検®準1級スーパーレベル問題集──本番がラクに解けるようになる』(テイエス企画)、『分野別IELTS単語集』(オープンゲート) などがある。

本書のご感想をお寄せください。
https://jtpublishing.co.jp/contact/comment/

英語を英語で理解する
英英英熟語 中級編

2022年11月5日　初版発行

編　者　ジャパンタイムズ出版 英語出版編集部＆ロゴポート
　　　　©The Japan Times Publishing, Ltd. & Logoport, 2022

発行者　伊藤秀樹

発行所　株式会社 ジャパンタイムズ出版
　　　　〒102-0082 東京都千代田区一番町2-2
　　　　　　　　　　一番町第二TGビル2F
　　　　ウェブサイト　https://jtpublishing.co.jp/

印刷所　日経印刷株式会社